THE COMPLIANCE ADVANTAGE

10 Must-Know Trends to Protect Your Investment Firm

By

Todd Cipperman, Esq.

The Compliance Advantage
Ten Must-Know Trends to Protect Your Investment Firm
by Todd Cipperman

Copyright © 2018 Todd Cipperman
Published by SkillBites LLC
www.skillbites.net

DISCLAIMER AND/OR LEGAL NOTICES

ISBN-10: 1-942489-67-6

ISBN-13: 978-1-942489-67-2

Acknowledgements

This book would not have been possible without the contributions of the team at Slice Communications, SkillBites, and Sarah Selverian. I would also like to thank the 7000+ readers of my daily blog who give me the motivation to get up every day at 5:00 AM to review the regulatory world and write a story. I also owe a debt to the clients I have served over my 25-year career; although I have dispensed much advice, I have learned much more from them. I would also like to express my deep gratitude to professional colleagues, friends, and mentors who have offered me invaluable encouragement, guidance, advice and straight-talk. Finally, and most importantly, I thank Jill Imparato, my wife and partner for nearly 30 years, who is my toughest critic and my fiercest advocate.

Table of Contents

To Jill, Olivia and Mary
for your support and encouragement and for the inspiration
you offer every day as writers, thinkers, and confidants.

Introduction and Summary

In January 2017, the new Trump administration promised a rollback of the regulatory state. What would be the impact on the investment management industry? Would the Republican-controlled Congress curtail or repeal the Dodd-Frank Act as proposed by Congressman Jeb Hensarling's CHOICE Act? Would "Too Big to Fail" become "Too Quick to Remember"? Would the regulatory state recede to levels last seen in 1973 or 1873? Would the public forget the abuses that led to the financial crisis? Would new SEC Chairman Jay Clayton turn the securities regulator away from enforcement and focus more on regulation and policy?

To echo Mark Twain, the death of financial regulation has been greatly exaggerated. Dodd-Frank remains the law of the land, Congressman Hensarling did not run for reelection, and control of financial legislation in the House of Representatives has changed hands. The Financial Stability Oversight Council and the Consumer Financial Protection Bureau remain in place. We have not seen any material changes to the Investment Advisers Act or the Investment Company Act. At the SEC, we have met the new boss, and, with regards to examinations and enforcement, he looks a lot like the old boss (to paraphrase The Who).

Investment management executives are left to wonder how to adjust to the current regulatory environment. They know they must designate a qualified chief compliance officer, adopt policies and procedures, and test those procedures every year. The SEC imposed these compliance obligations on all investment firms in 2004, and then Congress applied them to private fund firms as part of the Dodd-Frank Act in 2012. Whether by design or simply poor process, the compliance rules—206(4)-7 for advisers; 38a-1 for funds—leave much to the regulator's interpretation. From the very beginning, compliance professionals (whom I often refer to as "compli-pros") and lawyers have questioned what the SEC meant by "reasonably designed" policies and procedures and sufficient testing.

Over the last fifteen years, the SEC and the courts—through public statements, alerts, examination findings, and enforcement cases—have created a useful body of precedent. We now know that firms should retain a chief compliance officer who has relevant compliance experience and bandwidth, and not simply dual-hat the C-suite executive who drew the short straw at the management meeting. We know that firms should spend at least 5 percent of their revenues on compliance infrastructure. We know that policies and procedures should be somewhat voluminous, specific, and tailored to a firm's operating environment. We also know that testing should look more like an internal control review with specific forensic investigation and not just a quick meeting to ask if anybody knows of any compliance issues.

Faced with this ever-expanding mountain of information, investment professionals often ask me for help in understanding where they should focus limited resources. Executives receive legal treatises about this rule and that rule. They hear the SEC speak about this priority and that priority. They read headlines about cases that may or may not mean anything to them. Investment management professionals, most of whom simply want to run their businesses within the regulatory requirements, feel held hostage to changing standards and rules. They often must pay significant fees to outside professionals just to get a murky answer that offers little assurance that they will avoid a career-ending enforcement action. Unfortunately, no treatise can tell you all you need to know about compliance programs, and no degree program can train somebody to become a qualified chief compliance officer.

That's where this book comes in.

I share the same vision as most senior investment management executives: to create a reputable industry that allows firms to thrive and create value for investors. That's why, fifteen years ago, I founded Cipperman Compliance Services to provide best-in-class outsourced compliance services to firms that are not in a position to create their own compliance functions. We are twenty[1] professionals who have spent the vast majority of our careers designing and implementing compliance programs. Many of our senior professionals have

---

1   Due to hiring and attrition, the actual number may be more or less as of the date of publication. For a list of current professionals, please refer to our website: www.cipperman.com.

more than twenty years of experience in the investment management industry. Before I decided to start the law firm that evolved into this compliance services firm, I served as general counsel to a midsized asset manager and fund servicer; before that, I worked at a couple of Wall Street law firms. I attribute my intellectual curiosity to my parents and my great education at the University of Pennsylvania Law School and Cornell University. I have been reading the SEC's regulatory tea leaves for over twenty-five years.

Back in early 2008, I decided to start a daily blog about regulatory issues. I intended for the blog posts to offer investment management professionals a quick executive summary of a rule, statement, alert, or enforcement action so that they could have actionable information. Almost as an afterthought, I added "our take" about the subject matter so that executives could put the information into some context. This "Our Take," which allowed me some freedom to editorialize, also became the most popular part of the alerts. I have received tremendous feedback over the years indicating that the Our Take Alerts have been able to simplify complex information and offer an insightful view on regulatory issues. Today, my Alerts go to over 7000 people per day (via direct email, social media and website views). I have sent out more than 1500 alerts over the last 10 years.

I am thrilled that our readers appreciate the alerts. However, the readers have told me they want more. For the past several years, I have been giving an end-of-year speech at conferences and events that weaves together regulatory themes suggested by the prior year's Our Take Alerts. I have received great feedback that these thematic presentations have helped senior executives make sense of all the regulatory data they receive from other sources. They also like that I try to offer some advice and guidance rather than simply wag the finger at folks caught up in some unfortunate regulatory melee that could have been them were circumstances somewhat different.[2]

---

2   Generally, in our blog, I omit the names of respondents and defendants. The blog is intended to educate about principles, not to trade in gossip. However, we include the names in this book in an effort to expedite cross-referencing these cases for further research. Many of the subjects are excellent firms that made legitimate mistakes. Others probably settled cases for their own business reasons. Some are just wrongdoers. I have included the cases because of the principles they illustrate, not because I am commenting on the morality of the subject. If any of these firms takes offense, I apologize. If any of my friends or colleagues are hurt, please accept my explanation that it was unintentional and regrettable.

This book takes the next step. I have reviewed the Our Take Alerts from the last few years in an effort to come up with the ten most significant regulatory trends. I also offer some practical advice based on our combined experience operating investment management compliance programs. I believe that if you understand and address these ten trends, you will materially decrease your regulatory risk. This does not mean that I promise a clean SEC exam or exemption from an enforcement action. I do promise, though, that addressing these trends will significantly reduce your chances of a regulatory problem just as exercising and eating clean will reduce your risk of a major health problem.

I wrote this book for both senior executives and compliance professionals. I present the information in casebook format.[3] I offer a proposition or statement and then use redacted blog posts to illustrate, describe and prescribe. If you are a senior exec that only wants the big picture, ignore the blog posts and read the intros, summaries, and recommendations. If you are a compli-pro, you can use this book as a desk reference to research particular topics that affect your firm.

Why did I write this now, ten years after our first blog post? Because I hear a lot of "fake news" about the investment management regulatory environment. The election of Donald Trump has not meant the end of the SEC. In fact, his administration has not really focused on how the SEC supervises and regulates investment firms. I believe the current regulatory environment really began with Enron and the market-timing scandals of the early 2000s. These events—and the ensuing financial crisis and Madoff scandal—led to significant changes in the regulatory environment, how Congress and the public viewed financial wrongdoing, and the SEC's role in preventing such wrongdoing. The numbers of rules, enforcement cases, and examinations have steadily increased since 2003 regardless of the administration and SEC chairmanship. Mary Jo White may have trumpeted "broken windows" enforcement, but the William Donaldson SEC adopted the compliance rule, Christopher Cox presided over significant financial crisis cases, and Mary Schapiro helped

---

3   The blog posts are reprinted verbatim. Therefore, you should read them in the context of the date they were originally written. Sometimes, subsequent events may have changed the analysis. Also, you can go to the blog itself (www.cipperman.com/blog) to find the links to the underlying cases and orders.

implement Dodd-Frank. There is nothing to suggest that Chairman Clayton takes his obligation to protect investors any less seriously than his predecessors.

The SEC also changes slowly. Like most federal agencies, career civil servants carry out much of the SEC's day-to-day work, and many senior staff members have continued in their roles across multiple administrations. The political tone at the top may change slightly, but the real work continues in small offices throughout that large office building on F Street in Washington and all the regional offices. These career professionals provide welcome expertise and consistency to the investment management industry.

By its very definition, a book about trends relies heavily on recent events. Most of the blogs included in this book come from the last couple of years. Editorial limitations require me to leave out cases that you may feel are more important than others. Also, this book must go to press at some point, so significant events that occur after that date must wait until future posts, updates on our website, or our Second Edition, although I think the trends largely remain the same.

The Top Ten Investment Management Regulatory Trends (a Summary)

I have identified ten major trends that define the current investment management regulatory landscape based on my review of SEC and FINRA cases, statements, speeches, exam findings, and conference opinions. I believe that there may be other trends on the horizon (e.g., cryptocurrency), but I will muse on that in the last chapter of this book. Based on my practical experience, the ten most significant compliance trends are the following:

1. The SEC is examining more advisers and bringing more enforcement actions.

2. Senior executives are targeted for firm misconduct.

3. Securities markets service providers are charged with a market gatekeeping role.

4. Flimsy compliance programs are scrutinized and punished.

5. A super-fiduciary standard is challenging investment advisers.

6. Private equity firms are forced to transform their business practices.

7. Cybersecurity and protection of customer information have become top industry priorities.

8. Product marketers are re-assessing traditional marketing, distribution, and revenue-sharing.

9. Whistleblowers are encouraged to snitch on their employers and competitors.

10. FINRA has emerged as a securities enforcement power.

Although I will discuss each of these trends in depth, let's take a quick look at each of them.

Examinations and Enforcement

The SEC has continued the Obama administration's stated goals to increase examinations and enforcement activity. Chairman Clayton has committed to spending 50 percent of his budget on examinations and enforcement, which includes a stated goal to examine 20 percent of advisers per year. The SEC believes that enforcement, rather than piecemeal regulation, is the most effective regulatory tool to leverage limited regulatory resources. The numbers bear out this focus on examinations and enforcement. Fiscal year 2016 set historic records: 868 enforcement cases, including 160 against advisers, and $4 billion in disgorgement and penalties. Fiscal years 2017 and 2018 saw similar results. The SEC also keeps expanding its examination priorities: the 2018 Examination Priorities letter was sixteen pages long, as compared to the five-page letter in each of the prior three years.

Senior executive accountability

The SEC has made it a priority to target senior executives for securities markets wrongdoing. Through fiscal 2017, the SEC had charged individuals in more than 80 percent of standalone enforcement actions. The SEC, FINRA, and DOJ have made it their policy to hold investment management executives accountable for regulatory breakdowns.

Service providers as gatekeepers

Not content to limit their enforcement efforts to registrants and their executives, the regulators have brought many cases over the years against securities markets gatekeepers, including administrators, auditors, lawyers, consultants, underwriters, and custodians. Many of these cases have treated these service providers as the deep pockets liable for big fines and disgorgement after the primary actors have disappeared into insolvency.

Deficient compliance programs

Investment management firms really have no legitimate excuses for failing to adopt and implement a reasonable compliance program. Over the last fifteen years, a vast body of precedent has arisen for how to design and implement compliance programs. Additionally, an entire profession of compli-pros has grown up to advise, consult, and assist investment firms to comply with Rules 206(4)-7 and 38a-1. Yet, the SEC has found no shortage of compliance program deficiencies. In September 2017, the SEC's Office of Compliance Inspections and Examinations (OCIE) saw so many compliance problems during examinations that the staff felt compelled to issue a Risk Alert about the most pressing compliance issues. From OCIE's perspective, many registrants did not take their compliance obligations seriously. Compliance problems have moved beyond technical violations and into major cases, and the most egregious of these often have C-suite repercussions.

A super-fiduciary duty

Investment advisers have been subject to a fiduciary standard since 1940 through the Investment Advisers Act, which was initially intended primarily to root out conflicts of interest. In fact, most SEC enforcement cases against registered advisers allege some form of breach of fiduciary duty. In recent years, the SEC has raised the fiduciary bar in areas such as investment recommendations, best execution, pay-to-play, proprietary products, and fees. Recently, the SEC issued a modernized reinterpretation of a heightened fiduciary duty that stresses an adviser's duties of care, loyalty, best execution, and monitoring.

Private equity transformed

The Dodd-Frank Act brought private equity sponsors under the supervision of the SEC. The regulator has embraced this role, establishing a specialized unit within the Enforcement Division that has brought substantial cases involving longstanding practices by some of the largest and most venerable firms. Private equity firms now operate in a brave new regulated world where disclosure alone does not insulate self-dealing transactions. The regulator has questioned longstanding private equity practices involving broken deal fees, portfolio company consulting, expense allocations, and insider co-investments.

Cybersecurity

The SEC has emphasized the importance of protecting customer information from cybercriminals who seek to steal identities and misuse trading information. OCIE has conducted at least two acknowledged cybersecurity sweeps to make sure that firms have conducted vulnerability assessments and have taken action to protect customer data. In its most recent sweep, OCIE warned about template procedures, inadequate employee training, and questionable remediation procedures. Continuing to identify cybersecurity as a top compliance risk, the SEC created a dedicated Cyber Unit within the Enforcement Division to focus on market manipulation schemes, hacking, and the dark web. The SEC and FINRA have held several registrants accountable for their weak cybersecurity practices.

Marketing constraints

The SEC heavily scrutinizes how firms market their products, including how they pay for distribution or receive revenue sharing for the sale of third-party products. OCIE staff spend a great deal of time and effort verifying performance claims, ensuring that the adviser manages assets as advertised and doesn't lie about its credentials. The OCIE staff has warned advisers about misleading advertising and marketing practices. Although the law has not changed since the mid-1980s, OCIE staff have described a raft of advertising compliance misdeeds discovered during a 2017 sweep. Firms have failed to present performance net of fees, lied about GIPS (CFA Institute) compliance, and cherry-picked past recommendations to window-dress performance numbers.

Whistleblowers

Investment advisers better take insider complaints seriously because insiders with information have the ability to instigate SEC investigations. Underlying whistleblower cases is the SEC's belief that "Corporate officers have front row seats overseeing the activities of their companies." The Dodd-Frank rules prohibit retaliation against any person who becomes a whistleblower. Trying to encourage whistleblowers, the SEC prohibits any agreements that in any way restrict the rights of whistleblowers to come forward.

FINRA rising

Since the merger of NASD and the NYSE, FINRA Enforcement has shown ambitions to become the most feared securities cop on the beat, even though its big brother, the SEC, often gets more press coverage. One big difference is that FINRA is a nongovernmental organization that uses the fines it collects to help fund the rest of its operations.

* * *

Now that I have described the ten most significant regulatory trends affecting the investment management industry, let's take an in-depth look at all ten of these trends and what they mean for your organization....

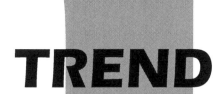

TREND

The SEC is examining more
advisers and bringing more
enforcement actions.

Thus far, Chairman Clayton has furthered his predecessor Mary Jo White's focus on increased examinations and enforcement with an emphasis on personal liability. Faced with continued criticism that the SEC only examines about 10 percent of registered advisers per year—as compared to FINRA, which annually examines about 40 percent of broker-dealers—Mr. Clayton committed to spending 50 percent of his budget on examinations and enforcement. He said he wants the SEC to examine 20 percent of advisers per year, which would blunt proposals to privatize adviser exams or create a new self-regulatory organization for advisers. The SEC continues to bring record numbers of enforcement cases even though the number of cases arising from the financial crisis have declined.

The numbers bear out this focus on examinations and enforcement. Fiscal year 2016 set historic records: 868 enforcement cases, including 160 against advisers, and $4 billion in disgorgement and penalties. In fiscal 2017, the SEC brought 754 cases and ordered $3.8 billion in penalties and disgorgement. Excluding the municipal disclosure initiative, the Enforcement Division filed more cases in 2018 than it did in 2016 and 2015, the last two years under the prior administration.

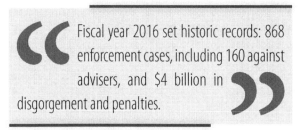

Fiscal year 2016 set historic records: 868 enforcement cases, including 160 against advisers, and $4 billion in disgorgement and penalties.

The SEC also keeps expanding its examination priorities. The 2018 examination priorities letter was sixteen pages long, as compared to the five-page letter in each of the prior three years. The SEC has promised to focus on retail investors, market infrastructure, FINRA, cybersecurity, and anti-money laundering. As the list expands over time, we wonder if anything is not a priority, especially when OCIE warns that its priorities list is "not exhaustive."

The greater likelihood of an SEC enforcement action looms as an existential threat to money managers and broker-dealers. A public enforcement action, whether won, lost, or settled, will cripple most firms. Simply being named in an enforcement case forces firms to reallocate limited resources to lawyers and forensic auditors while diverting management time and attention. Any resulting fines, disgorgement, penalties, and interest can be very expensive and are rarely covered by insurance. But, perhaps most troublesome is the resulting (and perhaps intended) effect on a firm's reputation. Once a firm receives the regulatory Scarlet Letter of a public enforcement action, institutional investors shy away as competitors use the action as a poisoned sword in every Request for Proposal process.

Even though an SEC action may have devastating effects on a firm, respondents/defendants usually roll over and settle because litigation is pointless. The SEC serves as police, prosecutor, judge, and jury. Administrative proceedings are adjudicated in front of administrative law judges appointed by the SEC itself. As a result, the SEC rarely loses a case. A 2014 *Wall Street Journal* twelve-month study reported that the SEC had won every case brought before an administrative law judge and 61 percent of its federal court cases. The federal government enjoys a significant resource advantage over private firms that do not have the taxpayers' backing.

The Supreme Court has tempered the SEC's advantage in recent years. In *Gabelli*, the Supreme Court ruled that the SEC must bring a civil enforcement action within five years of the alleged fraudulent conduct, rather than within five years of the date the SEC discovers the fraud. In *Kokesh*, the *Gabelli* precedent was extended to claims for disgorgement, finding that disgorgement was a "penalty" under *Gabelli*. Unfortunately, neither *Kokesh* nor *Gabelli* restrict voluntary SEC settlement agreements.

Even firms ready to fight often cower before the prospect of criminal prosecution. Although the SEC does not have criminal prosecution authority, it can – and often does – refer cases to the Department of Justice. Over the last several years, the DOJ has become creative in turning regulatory misdeeds into criminal prosecutions. For example, in *U.S. v. Cody*, the U.S. Attorney indicted an investment adviser for making a false declaration to the SEC during a sworn deposition. The Justice Department has also brought big cases under the Foreign Corrupt Practices Act, including a $413 million settlement with Och-Ziff. The Justice Department has also brought wrongdoers to justice based on the use of interstate emails (a predicate for mail/wire fraud), and anti-money laundering. Certainly, most senior executives would rather pay a civil fine than face time in a federal penitentiary. At the same time, the SEC uses the invocation of the Fifth Amendment's right not to testify for fear of self-incrimination to infer admitted civil liability.

While we all worry about the SEC and the DOJ, I would advise paying close attention to the state regulators. After all, way back in 2003 (under another Republican president), New York State Attorney General Eliot Spitzer launched the mutual fund market timing investigations that ultimately brought down several firms. The most significant difference between then and now is that the SEC views state regulators as enforcement allies with whom they share information and prosecution teams. The North American Securities Administrators Association (NASAA) has reported significant increases in civil and criminal penalties, especially against investment advisers. The Massachusetts Securities Division and the New York State Attorney General, wielding the Martin Act club, have been especially active.

Regardless of the rhetoric, firms must prepare for the advancing army of examiners and their enforcement cousins.

A. <u>SEC Priorities</u>. SEC Chairman Clayton continues the prior SEC's focus on examinations, enforcement, and personal liability.

SEC Filed 32% More Enforcement Cases Against Advisers and Funds in Fiscal 2018 (11/5/18)

The SEC Enforcement Division filed 32% more standalone enforcement cases against investment advisers and investment companies in fiscal 2018 (through September 30), as compared to 2017. Cases against investment advisers and investment companies (the second largest category) and broker-dealers (fourth largest) represented 35% of all standalone actions filed. Overall, the SEC Enforcement Division brought 490 standalone cases in fiscal 2018, a 10% increase over 2017. Excluding the municipal disclosure initiative, the Enforcement Division filed more cases than it did in 2016 and 2015, the last two years under the prior administration. The Enforcement Division obtained $3.9 Billion in penalties and disgorgement, which is consistent with amounts obtained during the prior several years. The Enforcement Division outlined five core principles, including a focus on individual accountability because "holding culpable individuals responsible for wrongdoing is essential to achieving our goals of general and specific deterrence and protecting investors by removing bad actors from our markets."

The Enforcement Division continues to pursue its active litigation agenda, especially against the investment industry. Apparently, the Jay Clayton SEC is not much different from the Mary Jo White

SEC when it comes to enforcement cases against adviser, funds, and broker-dealers.

SEC Chairman Re-Commits to Examinations and Enforcement (6/28/17)

In recent testimony about the SEC's proposed 2018 budget, Chairman Jay Clayton emphasized enforcement and examination activities. Mr. Clayton noted that 50% of requested budget resources will go to enforcement and examinations. He said that the SEC is on track to deliver a 20% increase in adviser examinations and plans a further 5% increase. He noted that the staff will put a special focus on cybersecurity efforts. Mr. Clayton also committed to continue the SEC's "vigorous enforcement efforts to investigate and bring civil charges" including critical areas such as "investment professional misconduct."

It appears that the Clayton SEC will continue the examinations and enforcement focus of the Mary Jo White SEC. The more things change, the more they stay the same.

SEC Examined 15% of Advisers Last Year and Wants to Expand Exam Program (5/1/18)

In recent testimony before Congress, SEC Chairman Jay Clayton reported that the SEC examined approximately 15% of all investment advisers in fiscal 2017, a 40% increase over the prior year. Mr. Clayton said that the SEC achieved these results through the reallocation of resources, advancements in technology, and "other efficiencies." He advocated for continuing to increase investment adviser coverage levels by requesting 24 additional positions in his 2019 budget request.

The SEC still falls short of FINRA who claims to examine 40% of broker-dealers per year. Perhaps, Chairman Clayton should reconsider requiring third party compliance reviews, a revenue-neutral policy idea, championed by former Republican Commissioner Dan Gallagher. Regardless, the chance of an exam continues to increase every year.

SEC Chairman Calls for Active Securities Enforcement (3/29/17)

Acting SEC Chairman Michael Piwowar strongly supports the SEC's use of enforcement as the mechanism to ensure fair capital markets that enable economic growth. In a recent speech, he said that "appropriate enforcement efforts" including a willingness to "assess penalties where appropriate and take back proceeds of fraud from the bad guys" facilitate capital markets by ensuring a fair and level playing field, thereby lowering the cost of capital. He also advocated for enforcement as the best way for regulators to focus "limited resources on a risk based approach to addressing the problems in the market, in contrast to burdensome and ultimately futile attempts to regulate away the problems." Mr. Piwowar also believes in complete and transparent disclosure but cautions against overregulation that impedes capital formation.

It does not appear that the new SEC administration will pull back from its heavy enforcement agenda that dominated the last several years. If anything, Mr. Piwowar suggests a greater enforcement push coupled with lesser regulation and enhanced disclosure.

SEC Filed Record Number of Enforcement Cases in Fiscal 2016 (10/13/16)

The SEC reported that it filed a record number of enforcement actions for its fiscal year ending September 2016, including the most ever cases against investment advisers and investment companies. The SEC brought 868 enforcement cases, exceeding the 807 it filed last year, including 160 against advisers and investment companies, which cases included eight significant cases against private equity firms. The SEC also cited its related cases against securities markets gatekeepers (e.g. attorneys, accountants, administrators), while noting the success of the whistleblower program, which awarded over $57 million to thirteen whistleblowers. The SEC obtained over $4 billion in disgorgement and penalties. SEC Chair Mary Jo White boasted, "By every measure the enforcement program continues to be a resounding success holding executives, companies, and market participants accountable for their illegal actions." She also explained that the SEC is "expanding the playbook, bringing novel and significant actions to better protect investors and our markets."

The SEC has become a litigation and enforcement machine rather than a traditional regulator. Focusing on the number of actions filed and penalties collected, the SEC will continue to use "novel" interpretations of the securities laws to ensure that it files ever more cases.

OCIE Releases 2018 Exam Priorities (2/8/18)

The SEC's Office of Compliance Inspections and Examinations[4] released its 2018 examination priorities, focusing on retail investors, market infrastructure, FINRA, cybersecurity, and anti-money laundering. As part of its mission to protect retail investors, OCIE will focus on (i) disclosure and receipt of compensation that could suggest a conflict of interest, (ii) robo-advisers, (iii) wrap fee programs, (iv) poor-performing mutual funds and ETFs, and (v) cryptocurrency offerings. OCIE also plans to supervise FINRA's "operations and regulatory programs" including the quality of its examinations. OCIE also intends to scrutinize cybersecurity and anti-money laundering practices including risk assessment and customer due diligence. OCIE makes clear that its priorities list is "not exhaustive" and could be expanded as a result of regulatory developments, examination information, complaints and tips, and other regulators.

OCIE is fairly transparent. Now that the staff has identified these issues, compli-pros should expect a heavy focus during examinations. Compliance departments should review policies and procedures and testing to get ready.

❏ The List: 2018 Examination Priorities

Both FINRA and the SEC OCIE staff released their 2018 examination priorities. This list synthesizes their missives into the 10 most significant regulatory priorities for investment management firms. Several of these priorities are new for 2018 including cryptocurrency, wrap fee programs, and thinly-traded securities. Others such as AML, suitability and best execution are regulatory greatest hits that appear nearly every year. Compli-pros should use these letters to prepare their compliance programs and exam readiness.

---

4   Referred to throughout as "OCIE".

Ten Most Significant 2018 Examination Priorities

1.	**Disclosure of fees and expenses:** Both OCIE and FINRA champion full transparency of fees and expenses so that clients can make informed decisions and understand possible conflicts of interest.
2.	**Cryptocurrency:** Expect a lot of attention paid to initial coin and cryptocurrency offerings including recommendations, disclosure, volatility, and security.
3.	**Cybersecurity:** The regulators want to ensure that firms implement adequate cyber policies and procedures to protect client information and data systems.
4.	**AML and KYC:** This is an area that both regulators have identified for many years, although the focus has moved to customer due diligence and firms' gatekeeper role to keep securities markets safe.
5.	**Protecting senior investors:** Both regulators want to protect senior investors. The SEC focuses on recommendations to retirement accounts. FINRA will review compliance with rules to prevent exploitation.
6.	**Wrap fee programs:** The SEC continues its persecution and prosecution of wrap fee programs, including due diligence, best execution, and conflicts.
7.	**Thinly-traded ETFs and microcaps:** The regulators have raised the red flag about recommending thinly-traded securities that are subject to market manipulation and pay exorbitant commissions.
8.	**High risk brokers:** FINRA wants firms to enhance hiring and supervision practices to keep bad actors out of the industry.
9.	**Suitability:** Firms must implement procedures to vet products and train reps.
10.	**Best execution:** FINRA is particularly concerned about order-routing practices and resulting conflicts of interest.

B.   Home Court Advantage. The SEC Enforcement Division almost always wins, although the Supreme Court has limited its lookback to five years.

WSJ Reports that SEC Has Won Every ALJ Case in Past 12 Months (10/27/14)[5]

The SEC has won every case it has brought before an administrative law judge through the 12-month period ending in September, according to

---

5   See also "SEC Wins With In-House Judges" (The Wall Street Journal 5/6/15)

a *Wall Street Journal* story (subscription required). By contrast, the SEC won only 61% of federal court cases during the same period. The *Journal*, quoting two SEC officials including Andrew Ceresney, the SEC's Director of Enforcement, asserts that that the SEC has shifted policy to try more cases before ALJs instead of proceeding in the federal courts. The *Journal* says the increased use of ALJs has occurred because of "enhanced powers" arising from the Dodd-Frank Act. The SEC appoints the ALJs, and the proceedings restrict testimony and evidence, as compared to federal court litigation.

 If the SEC accuses you of securities law violations, work hard to settle because you simply can't win if it goes to litigation. Given the new reality, the best course of action is to implement a robust compliance program to avoid any course of conduct that could lead to litigation.

Broker-Dealer Fined $1.25 Million for Deleting Phone Calls and Inadequate Records Retention (*In re BGC Financial*; 7/18/18)

The SEC fined a broker-dealer $1.25 Million for deleting recorded telephone conversations and failing to maintain books and records related to broker expenses. The broker-dealer deleted audio files after receiving an SEC request. The BD failed to "ensure that this litigation hold notice was distributed to the technicians in department responsible for maintaining voice recordings." The SEC also charges the firm with multiple failures to maintain required records of broker personal expenses and gifts and entertainment.

 The SEC will take punitive action against firms that fail to preserve regulatory records, whether or not the firm acted with bad intent. We recommend creating a regulatory records chart to serve as reference for all employees. Also, firms should create a policy and related procedures governing how it will ensure all employees comply with regulatory requests.

Broker-Dealer Fined for Failing to Produce Emails (*In re Industrial and Commercial Bank of China Financial Services*; 5/22/18)

The SEC fined and censured a broker-dealer for failing to produce requested emails as part of an enforcement investigation related to

9

potential money laundering activities. Despite repeated requests, the respondent could not produce emails for a 4-month period relevant to the subject activity. The firm initially represented that it produced all required emails, but ultimately found 40,000 missing emails from 30 employees maintained on a back-up email archive. The SEC noticed that the document production omitted emails from the correspondent firm through which the potential money laundering activity occurred. Rule 17a-4(j) of the Exchange Act requires broker-dealers to promptly furnish to the SEC any required records. The SEC also charged the firm with failing to file Suspicious Activity Reports.

Don't tell the SEC that you have complied with their document requests unless you have conducted adequate internal due diligence. The Enforcement staff will not look kindly on reckless or intentional misrepresentations during investigations. Also, lying to the staff can result in criminal penalties.

Supreme Court Limits SEC Disgorgement (*Kokesh v. SEC*; 6/6/17)

The U.S. Supreme Court has ruled that the SEC cannot seek disgorgement with respect to ill-gotten gains received more than 5 years ago. A unanimous Court held that disgorgement is a "penalty" under the statute of limitations because (i) the SEC brings public cases not intended to remedy individual harm and (ii) disgorgement is imposed for punitive and deterrent purposes. The Court rejected the SEC's argument that disgorgement is used for restitution because disgorgement orders often exceed the defendant's gains. The Court has previously held that SEC penalties are also subject to the 5-year statute of limitations.

The Supreme Court significantly constrains the SEC's enforcement power to demand huge settlements based on multi-year violations. The SEC will have to move more quickly to investigate and file.

Supreme Court Says That SEC Must Bring Actions within 5 Years of Fraud (*Gabelli v. SEC*; 3/1/13)

The U.S. Supreme Court has ruled that the SEC must bring civil enforcement actions within 5 years of the alleged fraudulent conduct rather than within 5 years of the date the SEC discovers the fraud. In a case involving alleged market timing, the SEC argued that it brought its civil enforcement case within the 5-year statute of limitations because it commenced the action within 5 years of discovery, even though the alleged market timing occurred more than 5 years prior. The SEC argued a fraud exception, where a victim has 5 years from the date of discovery. The Court disagreed, opining that a government agency is not similar to a private plaintiff seeking redress for fraud losses. The Court asserted that the central mission of the SEC is to root out fraud and has the resources (e.g. investigative and subpoena power) to discover it. Moreover, the SEC seeks penalties, not recompense for losses. Also, the Court stated that it would be very difficult to determine when a large government agency had knowledge of a fraud.

We have no problem with a tight statute of limitations for SEC actions. However, we do not agree with the Court's reasoning. Just because the SEC has the power to investigate doesn't mean it suspects (or should suspect) fraud is occurring with respect to all registrants. The unintended consequence of this decision is to encourage the SEC to file more enforcement actions just to make sure that it doesn't go past the 5 years.

C. Criminal Penalties. The SEC refers cases to the Justice Department when it believes the conduct warrants criminal penalties.

Adviser Indicted for Lying During SEC Deposition (*SEC v. Cody*; 10/9/17)

An investment adviser was indicted in part for making a false declaration in a court proceeding by lying to the SEC during a sworn deposition. The deposition occurred during an enforcement case that alleges that the adviser defrauded retirees by lying about account balances, falsifying documents, and creating false wires. According to the SEC, the adviser lied in a deposition about providing false documents to investors.

Once a formal enforcement proceeding commences, any misstatements under oath can lead to criminal proceedings for perjury or lying to a regulator. It's always wise to ensure that the lawyer defending the enforcement action has sensitivity to the possible criminal prosecution implications. An enforcement action may results in fines and industry bars, but criminal proceedings could result in jail time.

Adviser Jailed for Fraud Based on Emails that Crossed State Lines (*In re Holt*; 4/17/17)

A financial adviser was sentenced to 10 years in prison and ordered to make $2.9 Million in restitution because his emails that furthered his activities were transmitted over state lines, thereby constituting federal wire fraud. The SEC alleged that the defendant used cross-border emails and a web-based portal to provide false account statements and Ponzi-like payments. The SEC asserts that he misappropriated client funds by stealing their checks and depositing them into his bank account. The U.S. Attorney brought a criminal indictment against him for wire fraud based on the emails.

Federal wire fraud crime carries big prison and financial penalties. In this case, the U.S. Attorney leveraged the SEC charges into a federal conviction based on his cross-state emails.

Large Hedge Fund Manager and CEO to Pay $413 Million to Settle Bribery Charges (*In re Och-Ziff*; 10/4/16)

A large hedge fund manager and its CEO agreed to pay over $413 Million in civil and criminal penalties to the SEC and the Justice Department in connection with bribing foreign officials to invest sovereign wealth funds into the respondents' investment funds. The SEC asserts that the firm did not follow its own anti-corruption procedures by failing to conduct required enhanced due diligence when concerns were raised. Although the SEC does not accuse the CEO of knowing about the bribes, they fault him and the CFO for approving the transactions despite red flags and warnings. As part of the settlement, the firm must hire a dedicated CCO that does not have any other job at the company. The SEC and DoJ allege several violations of the Foreign Corrupt Practices Act, the Investment Advisers Act, and the Securities Exchange Act. The SEC's Enforcement Director admonished: "Senior executives cannot turn a blind eye to the acts of their employees or agents when they became aware of suspicious transactions..."

As firms go global to attract assets, the risk management infrastructure to ensure compliance with the FCPA and other laws (including laws of the local jurisdiction) must follow.

Failure to Remedy Compliance Violations Costs International Bank (*In re Bank Leumi*; 10/24/16)

A large global bank admitted wrongdoing and agreed to pay a $1.6 Million penalty, in addition to $3.7 Million in disgorgement, for failing to stop its illegal practice of providing broker-dealer and investment adviser services to U.S. clients without registering. The SEC charges the firm with servicing high-net worth private clients by having relationship managers travel to the U.S. to meet with current and prospective clients and provide advice and brokerage services. In addition, the firm maintained brokerage accounts, executed orders, handled customer funds, and provided account statements. According to the SEC, the firm was aware that it was violating U.S. law as far back as 2008 and adopted policies and procedures, but failed to halt its violative conduct until at least 2013. The respondent also executed a Deferred Prosecution Agreement with the Justice Department for related conduct.

Compliance doesn't stop at adopting policies and procedures. Firms must follow-through with implementation, especially after self-identifying legal violations. Merely "talking the talk" without "walking the walk" on compliance will result in a front-page enforcement action.

D. <u>State Regulators</u>. Even if the SEC backed away from its examination and enforcement agenda, the state regulators appear ready to take the lead.

State Securities Regulators Escalate Enforcement Activity (10/11/17)

The North American Securities Administrators Association (NASAA), the organization of state securities regulators, reported that state securities regulators imposed $914 Million in restitution, fines and penalties in 2016, as compared to $766 Million in the prior year. In its Enforcement Report, NASAA also reported significant increases in criminal penalties including incarceration and probation. The number of investigations and administrative actions also increased especially against investment advisers, which, according to NASAA, may be due to "heightened state interest in individuals and firms who have transitioned from broker-dealer registration to investment adviser registration in recent years." NASAA also reported significant information sharing with federal regulators.

Over the last several years, the state securities regulators have expanded examinations and enforcement along with the SEC and FINRA, making it much more difficult for any adviser or broker-dealer to avoid regulatory scrutiny. It's worth noting that many state securities regulators have criminal enforcement authority.

Massachusetts Alleges that Adviser Shouldn't Have Charged Performance Fee (*In re Moser Capital*; 10/20/17)

The Massachusetts Securities Division instituted administrative proceedings against an unregistered fund manager for unlawfully charging a performance fee in addition to misleading investors. The MSD asserts that the respondent unlawfully "householded" an elderly client's assets with a nephew with power of attorney in order to meet net worth thresholds required to charge a performance fee. Massachusetts law prohibits charging performance fees in violation of Rule 205-3 of the Advisers Act, which limits performance fees. In addition to other sanctions, the MSD seeks to prohibit the respondent from registering as an exempt reporting adviser.

Expect more cases like this where the state regulators take the enforcement lead. This is a rare case specifically alleging violations of the performance fee rule. Also, securities lawyers and compli-pros should take notice that (i) the Massachusetts statute makes it unlawful to violate an SEC rule that would otherwise apply only to SEC-registered advisers and (ii) the MSD seeks to prohibit federal exempt reporting adviser registration as a remedy.

NYS Attorney General Sues Investment Bank for Issuing MBS with Weak Due Diligence (*New York v. J.P. Morgan Securities*; 10/2/12)

The New York State Attorney General has filed a lawsuit against a large investment bank alleging "multiple fraudulent and deceptive acts" in connection with mortgage-backed securitizations sponsored by a purchased firm. Making several broad allegations, the New York State Attorney General essentially alleges that the defendant did not conduct sufficient due diligence on the underlying mortgages even though it hired a third party. The NYSAG argues that the defendant intentionally pressured the third party with volume and turnaround requirements to ensure weak due diligence. Although the alleged conduct occurred at a firm purchased by the defendant, the NYSAG argues that the defendant could not have purchased the MBS sponsor without a $29 billion loan from the Federal Reserve Bank of New York. The lawsuit, filed in New York State court, charges violations of New York State's Martin Act, which prohibits deceptive practices in securities transactions.

We think that the NYSAG makes a weak case. The defendant hired a third due diligence firm on which it relied, and the NYSAG does not suggest that the due diligence firm was somehow unqualified or incompetent. Also, it appears that the defendant purchased substantially all the assets of the predecessor firm, raising questions about whether the defendant is legally responsible for liabilities left at the purchased firm. Also, the generalized allegations do not allege a particular fraud or deception, but broadly assert that the defendant engaged in a systematic deceptive program. It is unclear whether such broad allegations will stand, even under New York State's Martin Act, one of the broadest and most ambiguous state securities law statutes. [6]

SEC Will Share Information with States for Securities Enforcement (2/23/17)

The SEC and NASAA, the organization of state securities regulators, have signed an information-sharing agreement, intended to facilitate monitoring of compliance with the new crowdfunding rules and "to guard against fraud." The parties have agreed to use non-public information "to inform any investigation, examination, proceeding, or civil action." The agreement will "strengthen collaboration among state and federal securities regulators" and assist "in monitoring and evaluating new and amended exemptions at the state and federal level."

This agreement is more significant that it appears. The state regulators have generally opposed relaxing the securities laws. The SEC, by agreeing to share, gives the state regulators free reign to assume primary responsibility for crowdfunding enforcement. State securities regulators, which can often be more aggressive than the SEC, could, through

---

6   The respondent agreed to pay $613 Million to New York as a part of a broader $13 Billion global settlement.

aggressive enforcement, undermine the original goal of the legislation, which was to facilitate capital raising.

CFTC and States Sign Information Sharing Agreement for Enforcement (6/12/18)

The Commodity Futures Trading Commission (CFTC) and the North American Securities Administrators Association (NASAA), the organization of state securities regulators, have signed an information sharing agreement intended to facilitate state regulators to investigate and enforce the Commodity Exchange Act. The Agreement also allows the CFTC to share information about state securities laws violations. The NASAA President described the unique role of state securities regulators because "they can bring enforcement actions for both securities law and commodities law violations" which is "particularly relevant given the recent epidemic of schemes involving cryptocurrencies and other modern types of commodities.

The MOU deputizes the state regulators to enforce the commodities laws, which helps the budget-strapped CFTC. It also continues the trend of more active state securities authorities.

FIVE ACTION ITEMS:

1. Conduct a mock audit to understand your examination weaknesses.

2. Engage with a regulatory law firm and a compliance services firm that can keep you informed of regulatory developments and prepare you for an exam.

3. Watch what you say during an examination. It's not a litigation, but it may become one.

4. Resolve regulatory problems, including reimbursing clients, before the SEC arrives.

5. Enhance areas that are more likely to induce criminal prosecution, such as anti-money laundering, Foreign Corrupt Practices, and insider trading.

TREND

2

Senior executives are targeted
for firm misconduct.

Financial executives, who feel like they have regulatory targets on their backs, are not wrong or paranoid. In fact, the SEC and the Department of Justice have stated policies to prosecute individual executives. Again following Mary Jo White's playbook, Chairman Clayton has identified individual accountability as a core enforcement principle because the ripple effect of fear deters wrongdoing by other executives. Last year, the SEC walked that talk as over 80 percent of enforcement cases charged an individual executive. The SEC has become creative in prosecuting corporate executives, using obscure statutes such as Section 20(b), which allows prosecution without directly linking a control person to the unlawful conduct.

Financial executives should also fear the long arm of former Deputy Attorney General Sally Yates, who left a far more significant legacy than refusing to enforce President Trump's travel ban. Ms. Yates was the primary driver for changing the DOJ enforcement manual to credit corporations for identifying individual wrongdoing. She identified individual accountability as the centerpiece of the DOJ's corporate enforcement strategy. Because of the Yates memo, corporations have an incentive to sacrifice their corporate executives to criminal prosecution. There has been no word as to whether the current administration plans any changes.

The regulators have carried through on their promise to prosecute individuals, bringing cases against CEOs, operations executives, portfolio managers, traders, in-house lawyers, compliance officers, and other rogue employees. Although compliance officers have seen their fair share of cases, the SEC will not allow advisers and broker-dealers to point the finger at the Chief Compliance Officer as the regulatory hall monitor responsible for every misdeed perpetrated by unruly employees. Instead, the SEC has properly put blame on the senior executives responsible for organizational wrongdoing, even if the enforcement lawyers can't prove specific personal benefit. Going further, the SEC has alleged direct securities law violations and breaches of fiduciary duty—charges that carry more significant penalties than alleging that a senior executive merely "caused" or "aided and abetted" the firm's violations. Very often, these individual charges result in permanent industry bars that effectively end the careers of the accused individuals.

The SEC has shown a willingness to bring cases against the C-suite. CEOs have been charged with ignoring firm policies and hiding transactions. In *SEC v. Blumberg*, the SEC and the DOJ charged a broker-dealer CEO with control person liability for heading a business that illegally routed orders to an offshore affiliate that charged undisclosed commissions. The prosecutors argued that the CEO knew of the misconduct, encouraged it, and helped hide it.

When the SEC brings cases against investment advisers, it nearly always names one of the firm's principals. In *Rafal*, an example of this type of case, the CEO of an investment adviser firm agreed to a six-figure fine and an industry bar for a series of regulatory violations, including lying to the SEC (which also led to criminal charges).

The SEC has not stopped at the C-suite. The Enforcement Division does not accept the "just doing my job" defense even if the respondent/defendant did not directly benefit from the wrongdoing. The SEC has brought cases against the head of regulatory reporting for miscalculating customer reserves (*In re Tirrell*), a middle office trader for helping to conceal commissions (*In re Nowak*), a chief accounting officer for approving CEO expense reimbursements (*In re Sabatino*), and an operations manager for helping her boss steal from clients (*SEC v. Bahgat et al*). The revered portfolio managers and traders, often more powerful than firm leaders, have also been charged with attempting to inflate their bonuses by lying about valuation and hiding personal conflicts (*See e.g. SEC v. Chan, In re Johns*).

> " The Enforcement Division does not accept the "just doing my job" defense even if the respondent/defendant did not directly benefit from the wrongdoing. "

In-house lawyers have incurred the special wrath of the Enforcement Division, which has argued that lawyers have a higher duty because of their unique knowledge and position. In *Diaz*, the SEC fined and barred a GC/CCO for failing to disclose unauthorized investments during meetings with clients. The lawyer's confidentiality and zealous advocacy obligations conflicted with her fiduciary responsibilities, highlighting the inherent conflict of serving as both GC and CCO. In *SEC v. RPM & Moore*, the GC/CCO was charged with failing to make fulsome disclosure to his superiors about a DOJ investigation.

The SEC has also brought several seminal cases during the last couple of years against compliance officers, whom the SEC has described as their designated private sector agents. In the *Young* case, brought against the CCO of Stanford

Trust, the SEC barred Mr. Young even though it is unclear what he knew about his firm's ongoing fraud. In *Blackrock and Battista*, the CCO was the only senior corporate executive charged when a portfolio manager engaged in a series of conflicted transactions. Similarly, only the CCO was charged and fined in *Haider*, which involved alleged anti-money laundering failures at MoneyGram. The SEC has also brought a number of cases against dual-hat executives who serve as CCO in addition to another corporate function.

Although some of these allegations against CCOs appear egregious, prosecuting the CCO can be counterproductive. Many CCOs have changed jobs or left the industry out of fear of personal liability—a trend that has exacerbated the current compliance talent shortage. We believe that the SEC should never prosecute the CCO unless the SEC can show that the CCO personally benefitted from the wrongdoing or helped further the unlawful conduct. Regardless, CCOs, like other executives, must concern themselves with a career-ending enforcement action by regulators intent on targeting individuals.

A. Core Enforcement Principle. Individual accountability is a core SEC enforcement principle.

SEC Enforcement Division Targets Financial Executives (11/17/17)

In its 2017 fiscal report, the SEC's Enforcement Division cites individual accountability as one of its core enforcement principles. The report expresses the Enforcement Division's view that "individual accountability more effectively deters wrongdoing." Since Chairman Clayton took office, the SEC has charged an individual in more than 80% of standalone enforcement actions. The report notes that it can be more expensive to pursue individuals, but "that price is worth paying." The report notes a modest decrease in filed enforcement actions and recoveries since 2016: 754 vs. 784 cases (excluding municipal cases) and $3.8 Billion vs. $4 Billion in total money ordered.

"Just because you're paranoid doesn't mean they aren't after you." (Joseph Heller) The data and the explanation imply that the SEC will prioritize prosecuting individuals, even if the money ordered is smaller than in institutional actions, because of the fear and deterrent effect. If financial executives need another reason to engage a best-in-class compliance program, how about protecting yourselves from a career-ending enforcement action?

White Says SEC is Innovating to Bring Actions against Individuals (5/21/14)

SEC Chair Mary Jo White, in a recent speech to a group of white collar criminal attorneys, stressed the importance of prosecuting individuals. She said that a corporation acts through individuals and that "if an enforcement program is to have a strong deterrent effect, it is critical that responsible individuals be charged." Ms. White cited statistics indicating that the SEC charges individuals in over 80% of its actions. Moreover, she said the SEC is looking for "ways to innovate in order to further strengthen our ability to charge individuals." As part of this innovation, she said the SEC will bring cases under Section 20(b) of the Exchange Act, which imposes primary liability on a person that acts through another person. She said the SEC will use Section 20(b) against those participating in the dissemination of misleading information to investors including offering documents and marketing materials. She also indicated that the SEC wants to step up the use of industry bars against individuals.

Every investment management executive should be concerned that enforcement actions will likely include actions against them personally and will likely include an industry bar, which is tantamount to a career death penalty.

Justice Department Will Focus on Prosecuting Individuals in Corporate Cases (11/18/15)

Deputy Attorney General Sally Quillian Yates said in a speech that the Justice Department has revised its Manual to focus on the prosecution of individuals in corporate cases. The revisions require companies that want credit for cooperating to provide "all non-privileged information about individual wrongdoing." The DoJ also amended the Manual to apply the same standards to its civil cases. The rationale for these changes is to "emphasize the primacy in any corporate case of holding individual wrongdoers accountable." Ms. Yates sought to explain and expand upon the DoJ's new policy "designed to ensure that individual accountability is at the heart of our corporate enforcement strategy" that was announced in September. Ms. Yates also recognized compliance officers as a "crucial partner" to combat corporate misconduct and cited the importance of "rigorous internal controls" that help companies "self-assess and self-correct."

It's not just the SEC that has increased focus on prosecuting individuals. The DoJ, which prosecutes corporate criminal cases, also seeks cases against individual corporate actors. Also, robust compliance programs help avoid career-ending (and potentially freedom-ending) actions against corporate officers.

SEC Creates Website to Search Enforcement Cases for Bad Actors (5/4/18)

The SEC has launched an online search tool that includes a database of all individuals who have settled, defaulted, or contested an SEC enforcement action that resulted in a final judgement or order in federal court or an administrative proceeding. The new system called SALI – SEC Action Lookup for Individuals – includes any respondent/ defendant and not just investment professionals. The current database extends back to 2014, although the SEC intends to expand the database.

The SALI database closes an information gap that made it cumbersome for investors to investigate charges against unregistered individuals. The system also facilitates research of wrongdoing by investment pros. This continues the regulators' expressed goal of weeding out bad actors from the securities industry.

B. <u>CEOs</u>. Firm leaders have faced charges for individual and firm wrongdoing.

Hedge Fund CFO Barred and Fined for Unauthorized Money Movements (*SEC v. Gruss*; 5/29/18)

The former Chief Financial Officer of a now-defunct hedge fund was fined and barred from the industry for authorizing improper interfund transfers and other financial improprieties. The SEC alleged that the

CFO authorized the ongoing transfers of funds from an affiliated offshore fund to facilitate the activities of a cash-strapped on-shore funds. The CFO continued the practice even after two subordinate accountants resigned after complaining that the practice did not comport with the funds' governing documents or applicable accounting standards. The SEC accused the CFO with aiding and abetting his firm's activities that defrauded investment advisory clients.

The SEC will seek to hold individual officers accountable for the illegal actions of the firms they manage. The SEC's Enforcement Division has cited personal accountability as a core enforcement principle.

BD CEO Faces Criminal and Civil Charges (*SEC v. Blumberg*; 8/8/14)

The Department of Justice has announced criminal charges and the SEC has initiated securities fraud charges against the CEO of a broker-dealer that routed orders to an offshore affiliate to capture undisclosed mark-ups and mark-downs.[7] In addition to securities fraud and aiding and abetting, the SEC has included a Section 20 claim against the defendant for control person liability. The SEC complaint alleges that the CEO knew of the misconduct, encouraged it, instructed employees how to hide it, and lied to clients. Andrew Ceresney, Director of the SEC's Enforcement Division warned, "We will continue to hold individuals accountable, including senior officials at broker-dealers, when they engage in fraudulent schemes to mislead customers." Stephen L. Cohen, Associate Director, explained that the defendant "directed a culture of deception and greed that systematically harmed investors. He had the power to put an end to this fraud, but instead used his power to encourage and perpetuate it."

SEC Chair Mary Jo White recently warned that the SEC intended to use Section 20 to prosecute high-ranking corporate executives.

---

7   Mr. Blumberg pleaded guilty to securities and wire fraud in August 2017.

CEO Hid Solicitation Payments and Then Lied to Clients and the SEC (*In re Rafal*; 1/10/17)

The CEO of an investment adviser admitted wrongdoing and agreed to pay over $575,000 and an industry bar for paying undisclosed solicitation fees. The CEO also faces criminal charges for misleading SEC enforcement investigators, thereby obstructing proceedings of a federal agency.[8] The respondent admitted to paying a lawyer-friend a referral fee without disclosure to the referred client as required by Rule 206(4)-3 of the Advisers Act. The pair conspired to conceal the payments through sham legal invoices. Upon hearing rumors of securities enforcement, the respondent sent false emails to clients claiming that the SEC had cleared the firm of any wrongdoing. The CEO's firm agreed to pay disgorgement but avoided more damaging penalties because it discovered the conduct, disciplined the CEO, and reported the conduct to the SEC. The lawyer-solicitor was also fined and barred from the industry.

Failure to disclose the solicitation payments would have resulted in a disgorgement penalty and enhanced disclosure. Lying to clients and the SEC triggered the criminal prosecution and the increased fines and industry bar.

C. <u>Operations Executives.</u> The SEC and FINRA will hold operations executives accountable, dismissing the "doing my job" defense.

Senior Execs and Firm Charged with Compliance Failures (*In re Wedbush*; 6/12/14)

The SEC has commenced enforcement proceedings against a large broker-dealer and two senior executives for failing to implement required compliance procedures for its sponsored access business.[9] The SEC alleges that the firm allowed unfettered market access to foreign trading firms without the required compliance controls relating to naked short sales, wash trades, manipulative layering, and money laundering. The SEC says that the two executives responsible for the unit had responsibility

---

8 The defendant was ultimately fined and sentenced to one year of probation.

9 The firm agreed to pay a $2.4 Million fine. Each of the executives settled for a $25,000 fine and $25,000 in disgorgement.

for implementing the required compliance controls. The SEC also alleges that the firm and the executives had adequate notice of the deficiencies after several regulatory actions against the firm's clients, an SEC exam deficiency letter, and meetings with SEC staff.

The SEC is holding senior executives, rather than compliance staff, accountable for failure to implement required compliance procedures. The SEC notes that the two senior executives gained financially by the business unit's success. In our view, the SEC is placing responsibility where it belongs i.e. with the senior executives that run the firm rather than compliance officers without a financial stake in wrongdoing.

SEC Takes Action against Head of Regulatory Reporting (*In re Tirrell*; 9/5/17)

The SEC issued a cease and desist order against the Head of Regulatory Reporting of a large investment bank for causing violations of the firm's customer protection rule. As previously reported,[10] the firm agreed to pay $415 Million to settle the charges. The SEC faults the respondent, who also served as the Financial and Operational Principal, with misleading regulators about the true purpose of certain synthetic transactions intended to reduce the amount held in the firm's reserve account. The SEC cites FINRA's handbook which prohibits any window dressing designed to reduce the reserve formula.

It is noteworthy that the head of Regulatory Reporting was the only individual specifically charged by the SEC in this action even though the firm paid a staggering settlement. Regulatory officers, including CCOs and FINOPs, continue to be targeted by the regulators.

Operations Manager Charged with Aiding/Abetting Securities Fraud (*SEC v. Bahgat and Colangelo*; 10/10/17)

The SEC accused the operations manager of a state registered investment adviser of aiding and abetting her boss's fraud by impersonating clients

---

10   See "SEC Takes Action Against Head of Regulatory Reporting" at https://cipperman. com/2017/09/05/sec-takes-action-head-regulatory-reporting/

to gain online account access. The SEC maintains that the operations manager, under the direction and the supervision of the firm's principal, telephoned a broker and impersonated a client to create on-line access to client funds that the principal ultimately misappropriated as part of a broader scheme involving almost $400,000 in client funds. The principal, also a defendant in the enforcement action, has left the United States. The SEC charges that the operations manager "knew or recklessly disregarded" that her boss's conduct "was improper and knowingly rendered…substantial assistance."

Don't help your boss commit securities fraud. There is no "dutiful assistant" or "just following orders" defense, whether or not the SEC can show you personally benefitted. In this case, the trusty assistant was left holding the liability bag when her boss fled the country.

Chief Accounting Officer Barred and Fined for Approving CEO Expenses (*In re Sabatino*; 11/20/17)

The SEC barred and fined a public company Chief Accounting Officer for approving undisclosed expense reimbursements for the company's CEO. The CEO ultimately repaid the $11.285 worth of perquisites incurred over a 5-year period for personal items such as private aircraft usage, cosmetic surgery, cash for tips, medical expenses, charitable donations, and personal travel expenses. The SEC asserts that the CAO approved the expenses in violation of company policy and without appropriate backup documentation and then failed to disclose the reimbursements in the company proxy statements. The SEC charges the CAO with causing the company to file false reports.

We wrote on Friday that the SEC is looking to hold financial executives accountable (see https://cipperman.com/2017/11/17/sec-enforcement-division-targets-financial-executives/). In this case, the SEC doesn't even allege that the CAO derived any personal benefit by approving his boss's expenses. Regardless, the SEC holds him accountable for allowing wrongdoing to occur.

D. <u>Portfolio Managers and Traders</u>. Star PMs and traders have been targeted.

CMBS Trader Lied to Clients about Pricing (*SEC v. Chan*; 5/16/17)

The SEC fined and barred an investment bank's head CMBS trader for lying to customers about pricing, spreads, and compensation over a 2-year period. According to the SEC, the defendant oftentimes used elaborate stories and doctored documents to support his untrue statements. The SEC asserts that clients relied on the incorrect information when making purchase/sale decisions. The SEC maintains that the respondent knowingly ignored compliance policies requiring truthfulness in dealings with customers. The defendant benefitted through higher discretionary bonuses resulting from his illicit activities, thereby making him directly liable for securities fraud.

OUR TAKE

It is noteworthy that the SEC took action against the trader himself rather than his firm, which presumably avoided liability because it had implemented adequate policies and procedures. SEC Commissioner Piwowar has previously indicated that the SEC should pursue individuals rather than firms.

Portfolio Manager Barred/Fined for Lying to CCO (*In re Johns*; 8/28/13)

A fund portfolio manager was barred from the industry and fined over $350,000 for misleading the Chief Compliance Officer investigating personal trading violations. According to the SEC, the respondent engaged in active personal trading in violation of Rule 17j-1 and the funds' Code of Ethics. The SEC alleges that the respondent did not pre-clear or report personal securities transactions, submitted false quarterly and annual reports, physically altered brokerage statements, and backdated confirmations. When the CCO inquired about irregularities, the portfolio manager falsely stated that certain brokerage accounts were closed and physically altered brokerage statements to hide his personal trading, as alleged by the SEC. The SEC charges violations of Section 17(j) and Rule 38a-1(c), which prohibits a fund officer, director, or employee from misleading the fund's CCO.

Compliance is not a cat-and-mouse game where those regulated try to evade the CCO. Rule 38a-1(c), as applied in this case, make clear that compliance is everybody's responsibility. We applaud the SEC for applying the compliance rule to the individual wrongdoer, rather than targeting the CCO for failing to stop the violations.

Portfolio Manager Made Personal Loan to CEO to Get on Board (*In re Louie*; 7/17/18)

A portfolio manager of an activist investment firm failed to disclose a $3 Million personal loan to the CEO of a company in which he invested. The portfolio manager made the loan, according to the SEC, to secure the CEO's support for his election to the Board as part of a broader initiative to exert control over the company. The SEC asserts that the portfolio manager violated his fiduciary duty to his clients by concealing his personal interest and that the investment manager failed to file a Schedule 13D (indicating more than passive investment). Also, the SEC faults the adviser for failing to implement a reasonable compliance program because the policies and procedures "did not discuss conflicts of interest more broadly in sufficient depth so as to capture and train employees to recognize other violative conduct not specifically identified."

Because portfolio managers are often treated like the rock stars of investment management, compli-pros must implement heightened supervision to protect against reckless actions that will ultimately hurt the firm. Procedures should include reviews of investment decisions, due diligence about personal dealings, reviews of transactions outside the ordinary course, and training all employees how to identify unlawful activity.

E. <u>In-House Counsel.</u> In-house lawyers have a higher standard of care than other employees.

GC/CCO Fined and Barred for Failing to Disclose Unauthorized Use of Funds (*In re Diaz*; 7/12/16)

The SEC censured, fined and barred from practicing before the Commission the General Counsel/Chief Compliance Office of an investment adviser accused of making unauthorized investments and then misleading a public pension client. The SEC alleges that the GC/CCO, also an 8% equity participant in the adviser, knew about the transactions but failed to disclose them to the public plan client on several occasions including an annual budget meeting. The SEC asserts that a "vast majority of the compensation earned by [the firm's] principals was directly attributable to the management and transaction fees" earned from its work with the public plan. The SEC charges the respondent with aiding and abetting securities fraud.

This is why a GC should not also serve as the CCO. Part of a lawyer's job is to advocate for his/her client and includes an absolute obligation to keep information confidential to preserve attorney-client privilege. The CCO is a regulatory officer whose job is to implement policies and procedures reasonably designed to prevent violations of the securities laws and report on the compliance program. These two conflicting obligations cannot coexist in the same office.

SEC Charges In-House General Counsel with Failed Disclosure (*SEC v. RPM and Moore*; 9/14/16)

The SEC has charged the general counsel/chief compliance officer of a public company with failing to disclose material losses relating to a DoJ investigation. The SEC accuses the lawyer, who had responsibility for responding to the government investigation, with failing to disclose material facts to the company's CEO, CFO, audit committee and independent auditors. The SEC maintains that proper disclosure should have resulted in disclosure of a loss contingency or recording of an accrual on the company's financial statements. The SEC asserts that the GC/CCO held back material facts about the investigation because he held $1.8 Million in the company's stock, knew that public disclosure would hurt the firm's business and reputation, and felt pressure not to disclose extraordinary charges on financial statements.

Even lawyers do not have immunity from the SEC's policy of holding senior executives accountable for corporate wrongdoing. It is unclear how the SEC will calculate the defendant's ill-gotten gains, but the fact that the SEC specifically cited the defendant's stock ownership may serve as the basis of a disgorgement order.

F. <u>Chief Compliance Officers</u>. The regulators have targeted CCOs for dereliction of duty.

SEC Affirms Industry Bar and Financial Penalties against Chief Compliance Officer (*In re Young*; 4/4/16)

The SEC upheld an Administrative Law Judge's decision against a Chief Compliance Officer related to his participation in a Ponzi scheme. The SEC upheld penalties including an industry bar, disgorgement of compensation, and fines. The SEC held that the CCO acted at least negligently in approving marketing materials that contained unverified statements despite numerous red flags raised by regulators, clients, and a clearing broker. The respondent also served as the firm's "due diligence officer" with responsibility for verifying statements in marketing materials. The SEC rejected the respondent's claim of immunity because of his role as CCO, citing an FAQ about Failure to Supervise liability for broker dealers: "A compliance role does not preclude liability where the respondent engages in conduct that 'otherwise violate[s] the securities laws or aid[s] and abet[s] or cause[s] a violation.'" The SEC criticizes the respondent for his failure to carry out his due diligence responsibilities by stating that it was his "actions and failures to act, not his designation as chief compliance officer, that is the basis for his liability."

This is a very troubling precedent for CCOs, despite the damaging set of facts presented. The SEC could have found liability solely because the respondent served as an officer of the company and continued to help create and approve marketing materials in the face of obvious red flags. However, the SEC went further by suggesting that it need only prove that a CCO acted negligently with respect to the duties undertaken. Moreover, the SEC points to its failure to supervise standards utilized in broker-dealer regulation to determine where compliance ends and management begins.

CCO Sanctioned and Firm Fined $12 Million for Allowing PM Conflict of Interest (*In re Blackrock and Battista*; 4/21/15)

The SEC censured and fined a Chief Compliance Officer and fined his employer, a large mutual fund adviser, $12 Million for permitting, and then failing to report to fund boards, a portfolio manager's outside business activities. According to the SEC, the PM managed several energy-focused funds and reported his interest in a family-owned energy-related company. The family company entered into a joint venture with a company held by the registered funds. The SEC charges that the CCO and other members of the firm knew about the activity and allowed it to continue in violation of its own policies. The SEC also faults the firm for failing to inform the fund boards or its advisory clients about the conflict of interest. Moreover, the firm failed to implement reasonable compliance policies and procedures by failing to follow-up on firm-imposed restrictions or implement policies and procedures to monitor the activities which expanded over time. The SEC charges the firm with breaching its fiduciary duty and violating the compliance rules (206(4)-7 and 38a-1). "This is the first SEC case to charge violations of Rule 38a-1 for failing to report a material compliance matter such as violations of the adviser's policies and procedures to a fund board," according to Julie M. Riewe, Co-Chief of the SEC Enforcement Division's Asset Management Unit. The SEC notes that the conflict of interest was uncovered in a *Wall Street Journal* article.

How does this happen at a large asset manager with an experienced team of legal and compliance professionals and independent boards? Lack of independence. All firms should conduct a third party assessment of its compliance activities, including a review of conflicts of interest, to ferret out longstanding practices that internal personnel accept as part of the culture.

CCO Barred and Fined $250,000 for AML Compliance Breakdowns (*U.S. Dept of Treasury v. Haider*; 5/9/17)

The Chief Compliance Officer of a money transmitter agreed to pay a $250,000 penalty and accept a 3-year bar from serving in a compliance function in connection with anti-money laundering compliance failures. As part of his settlement with FinCEN and the U.S. Attorney, the CCO also admitted to failing to stop potential money laundering despite being "presented with information that strongly indicated that the outlets were complicit in consumer fraud schemes" and implementing an inadequate AML program. The settlement concludes the case which had initially imposed a $1 Million fine, which could have been as much as $4.75 Million based on the statutory penalty of $25,000 for each failure to file a Suspicious Activity Report. The Acting U.S. Attorney explained the decision to prosecute a CCO: "Compliance officers perform an essential function, serving as the first line of defense in the fight against fraud and money laundering."

Compliance officers that assume anti-money laundering duties are subject to prosecution and significant fines by both FinCEN and the DoJ (in addition to FINRA and other financial regulators). Nobody condones the CCO's conduct in this case, but one question many compli-pros have asked is why has the CCO been singled out for personal liability? Why didn't the feds pursue the operations folks that vet clients or the senior executives in charge? And, why does the CCO pay a fine when he did not financially benefit from the misconduct?

CCO Blamed for Signing Certifications That Facilitated Unlawful Securities Lending (*In re Ryan*; 8/2/18)

The SEC censured and fined the Chief Compliance Officer of a broker-dealer for signing certifications that she knew, or should have known, were inaccurate, thereby enabling her firm to engage in unlawful securities lending transactions. The CCO signed certifications to third party depositaries that confirmed her firm complied with certain ADR prerelease agreements that required that her firm hold ordinary shares that evidenced ADRs. The SEC maintains, however, that the CCO knew the firm did not comply with those agreements because she participated in drafting the firm's procedures for acquiring prerelease ADRs and knew that the firm did not comply with the prerelease agreements. The SEC charges the CCO with causing her firm's violations of the Exchange Act's antifraud provisions.

Compliance officers should avoid signing certifications that facilitate securities transactions. If the situation requires a certification, a CCO must conduct adequate due diligence to ensure the accuracy of all statements made. Also, we would recommend that a CCO obtain back-up certifications from others in the organization.

Compliance Officer Charged with Securities Fraud (*In re Bull et. al.*; 3/15/18)

The SEC charged a compliance officer with securities fraud and aiding and abetting his employer's violations by "adding an aura of legitimacy" to an oil and gas offering fraud. The SEC accuses the compliance officer of ignoring misstatements in offering documents and client communications and with failing to conduct required investor eligibility due diligence. The SEC also charges the compliance officer with filing false Form Ds with the Commission.

This is what we call "compliance alchemy" i.e. using purported compliance as a tool to further securities law violations. The SEC has become wise to firms that implement sham compliance programs.

SEC Fines and Bars CCO for Ignoring Compliance Problems (*In re Southwind*; 12/27/17)

The SEC fined and barred an adviser's Chief Compliance Officer from acting in a compliance or supervisory capacity because of his failures to remedy compliance deficiencies. The adviser hired an outside compliance consultant which recommended 59 compliance action items. The SEC alleges that the CCO failed to address many of the issues raised including failures to (i) ensure a surprise audit pursuant to the custody rule, (ii) retain emails and other electronic records, and (iii) implement policies to protect customer information. The SEC also charges the CCO with compliance program deficiencies including failures to update the compliance manual or conduct any meaningful annual review of the compliance program. The firm's president/principal was also censured and fined.

The SEC doesn't often prosecute standalone (i.e. not dual hat) CCOs without an underlying client loss, but it will if the CCO ignores obvious compliance deficiencies of which he has notice. This is what we call "compliance alchemy" i.e. an appearance of compliance infrastructure without an effective program. This CCO had a compliance manual, did some quarterly testing, and hired a third party consultant. But, neither the CCO nor the firm took any action to actually implement relevant procedures to address cited compliance deficiencies.

❑ *The List: The Seven Most Important Attributes of a Chief Compliance Officer*

The Seven Most Important Attributes of a Chief Compliance Officer

1.	**Regulatory Knowledge**—A CCO must have an in-depth knowledge of the laws, regulations, interpretations, and regulatory positions as well as the firm's compliance policies and procedures and their implementation.
2.	**Firm Knowledge**—A CCO must become intimate with the firm's organization, finances, clients, and culture.
3.	**Industry Experience**—An effective CCO must advise his/her firm's executives about how other industry players implement products, develop structures, work with the regulators, and utilize technologies.
4.	**Analytical Intelligence**—Dynamic firms in dynamic markets require a CCO that can be flexible enough to adopt new approaches, yet professionally skeptical of unproven methods, products and structures.
5.	**Diplomacy**—Knowledge and experience will only go so far if a CCO does not have the political skills to convince business executives.
6.	**Calmness**—A CCO must always display grace under pressure and show confidence regardless of the situation and implications.
7.	**Fearlessness**—A CCO must exercise independence with senior executives and put personal issues aside while tackling difficult issues, even in the face of possible personal liability.

G. <u>Rogue Employees</u>. The regulators target individuals, rather than their employers, when they ignore compliance policies.

Financial Adviser Barred for Using Personal Emails/Texts (*In re Parthemer*; 3/15/17)

A financial adviser was barred from the industry for using personal email and text messages as part of an unlawful scheme to solicit client investments. The SEC alleges that the financial adviser failed to submit personal communications that concerned brokerage business to his broker-dealers as required by the firms' policies and procedures. The SEC has charged the respondent with aiding and abetting the broker-dealers' violations of their obligations to retain emails and other client communications. The SEC maintains that the adviser sold securities to clients without conducting adequate due diligence or providing sufficient disclosure about the offering or his conflicts of interest.

This case is a good example of the SEC properly asserting individual accountability rather than only punishing their organizations. Every employee at a regulated entity should have a regulatory responsibility to assist with securities laws compliance, and the regulators should prosecute individuals who intentionally evade internal policies to further wrongdoing.

SEC Upholds FINRA Bar Based on Untruthful Form U4 (*In re Riemer*; 11/7/17)

The SEC has upheld a statutory disqualification imposed by FINRA for failing to file a truthful U4 and lying on compliance questionnaires. FINRA barred the appellant from the securities industry because his Form U4 failed to disclose federal tax liens and a bankruptcy, and because he provided false responses on his firm's annual compliance questionnaires. The appellant sought a stay of the disqualification on the grounds that he would get fired from his current job and suffer economic harm. The SEC rejected his argument and denied the appeal because FINRA has an interest in protecting investors, and a stay of the statutory disqualification for material failures on Form U4 "could endanger investors."

FINRA and the SEC take Form U4 (and annual compliance questionnaires) very seriously. The regulators view the disclosure as a lynchpin to protecting investors.

FIVE ACTION ITEMS:

1. Ensure the compliance and supervision function includes reviews of C-suite activities.

2. Hire a dedicated and experienced Chief Compliance Officer.

3. Separate the legal function from the compliance function.

4. Do not offload compliance implementation on business unit heads.

5. Buy insurance for directors and officers.

TREND

3

Securities markets service
providers are charged with a
market gatekeeping role.

In the *Lincoln Savings and Loan* case, involving a widespread S&L fraud perpetrated by Charles Keating and company, Judge Stanley Sporkin (a former director of the SEC's Division of Enforcement) pondered how the alleged fraud could possibly have occurred given the army of lawyers and accountants involved. In his opinion, he asked:

> "Where also were the outside accountants and attorneys when these transactions were effectuated? What is difficult to understand is that with all the professional talent involved (both accounting and legal), why at least one professional would not have blown the whistle to stop the overreaching that took place in this case."

Since Judge Sporkin's famous rhetorical question, the SEC has sought to hold gatekeepers accountable for the misconduct of their clients. It has not been easy. For the most part, gatekeepers such as administrators, custodians, consultants, and lawyers are not registrants subject to SEC supervision. Even auditors avoided direct SEC scrutiny until the Enron scandal, which gave rise to the Sarbanes-Oxley Act and the Public Company Accounting Oversight Board. Lawyers, auditors, and custodians have successfully convinced Congress and the public that SEC involvement was unnecessary because other regulators already did the monitoring.

In the absence of specific laws or rules to address the liability of securities markets service providers, the SEC has become creative. Early cases alleged that the gatekeeper "aided and abetted" the registrant's misconduct. Later actions alleged that the gatekeeper "caused" the conduct. More recently, the SEC Enforcement Division has alleged that nonregistered service providers have a direct duty to aggrieved investors by way of some sort of fiduciary penumbra. The SEC has also used a very aggressive interpretation of "investment advice" to bring unsuspecting service providers under the full weight of the Advisers Act.

> " Very often, the administrator, auditor, or custodian has the deep pockets that remain after the undercapitalized primary violator disappears into bankruptcy or incarceration. "

These cases against gatekeepers are no small matters. Very often, the administrator, auditor, or custodian has the deep pockets that remain after the undercapitalized primary violator disappears into bankruptcy or incarceration. The SEC has imposed significant disgorgement and restitution orders on service providers to ensure that the government gets its prosecutorial full measure.

Despite the weak legal reasoning and large penalties, it just doesn't make much sense for service providers to fight. In a competitive environment, it makes business sense to pay the fine and move on rather than to allow your competitors to use the uncertainty against you during the inevitable RFP process. The SEC is also correct that most of the gatekeepers have significant resources, making the fines and penalties a line item cost of doing business.

Over the last few years, the SEC has become active in all major service provider categories.

The SEC has targeted fund administrators although they are not registered and thereby directly subject to SEC supervision. In *Gemini Fund Services*, the SEC fined the fund administrator $560,000 for failing to uncover its client's fake loan fraud even though the third-party custodian ultimately confirmed the loan valuations. In *Apex Fund Services*, the SEC fined the fund administrator $350,000 for ignoring red flags about its client's unauthorized transactions, thereby enabling the scheme. The SEC has focused special attention on administrator-sponsored, mutual fund series trust platforms, bringing cases alleging failure to conduct due diligence on client compliance programs (*In re Northern Lights*) and faulty auditor independence due diligence (*In re ALPS*).

Although auditors are technically regulated by the PCAOB, the SEC Enforcement Division has expanded the auditors' gatekeeping responsibilities beyond Sarbanes-Oxley obligations. The SEC has blamed auditors for a wide range of conduct, including violations of the custody rule (*In re Santos, Postal & Co.*) and inflated valuations (*In re Summit Asset Strategies*). Auditor independence continues to be an SEC focus (See, e.g., *In re Ernst & Young*).

The government litigators have also expanded the "mob lawyer" doctrine by holding lawyers accountable for furthering fraud even though they may not have received proceeds from the unlawful conduct (other than their legal fees). A good example is the recent prosecution in the Martin Shkreli case where the SEC charged the lawyer with securities fraud for negotiating consulting agreements that documented the allegedly fraudulent transactions. In *Lynch*, the SEC asserted that the outside lawyer failed to conduct proper due diligence of a municipal bond offering. In *Schneider & Wilson*, the SEC accused the lawyers of issuing unsubstantiated legal opinions that facilitated blank-check company schemes. In *Flom & Schmidt*, the lawyers allegedly received funds on behalf of their Ponzi-scheming client.

Outside compliance consultants have also faced the SEC after failing to perform as required. In *Parallax*, the SEC alleged that the outside compliance consultant spent less than nine hours per month on his client's deficient compliance program, which failed to properly address principal transactions, the code of ethics, or the custody rule. In *Aegis Capital*, the outside consultant failed to take any action to verify the client's assets under management as reported on Form ADV.

A. Administrators. Fund administrators have been spotlighted for allowing clients to engage in unlawful conduct.

Fund Administrator Pays for Client's Fraud (*In re Gemini Fund Services*; 1/24/18)

A fund administrator agreed to pay over $560,000 to settle charges that it caused its client's violations of the Advisers Act's antifraud provisions. The client defrauded clients (and ultimately went to prison) for misappropriating client assets by creating fake loans in which the fund invested. The fund's custodian declined to book the fake loans because they lacked sufficient backup documentation. Regardless, the administrator included the loans in the fund's NAV even though, according to the SEC, it knew that the custodian excluded the loans. The SEC faults the administrator for failing to further investigate, notify the board or shareholders, or exclude the loans from the NAV calculation.

Although it may be a legal stretch to assert that a fund administrator caused a fraudulent client's illegal conduct, the SEC will hold securities markets gatekeepers accountable for their client's behavior. Service providers must conduct due diligence before accepting a client or risk being found guilty by association.

Fund Administrator Liable for Miscalculating Fund NAV (*In re SEI Investments Global Fund Services*; 4/27/18)

The SEC fined and censured a fund administrator for causing a money market fund's violations of the Investment Company Act. The SEC asserts that the administrator used a flawed valuation methodology that resulted in violations of Rule 2a-7. The fund was used as a vehicle to invest securities lending collateral for the benefit of affiliated mutual funds. Because the fund failed Rule 2a-7, the investments by the registered funds violated the affiliated transaction rules.

As was the case with another recent case against a fund administrator, the SEC will broadly interpret the securities laws to hold non-registrant service providers accountable as gatekeepers of the securities markets.

Fund Administrator Charged/Fined for Causing Client's Securities Fraud (*In re Apex Fund Services*; 6/20/16)

A private fund administrator agreed to appoint an Independent Compliance Consultant and pay more than $350,000 in disgorgement, fines, and interest to settle charges that it caused its clients' securities fraud. The SEC asserts that the respondent "ignored clear indications of fraud" including undisclosed brokerage and bank accounts and unauthorized principal borrowing, about which, the SEC avers, the firm had knowledge but failed to adequately adjust disclosures and reports. Andrew Ceresney, Director of the SEC's Division of Enforcement, stressed that "administrators are responsible for ensuring that fund records provide accurate information about the value and existence of fund assets" and that the administrator "failed to live up to its gatekeeper responsibility and essentially enabled the schemes to persist at each of these advisory firms until the SEC stepped in."

Bad clients put significant strain on industry service providers, including regulatory scrutiny. When the SEC uses the term "gatekeeper," it implies a duty to keep questionable managers out of the industry. Otherwise, the service provider will face regulatory action for causing the securities violations.

Fund's Trustees and Administrator Faulted for Inadequate Compliance Program (*In re Northern Lights*; 5/3/13)

A mutual fund's compliance program violated the fund compliance rule (38a-1) because the trustees did not receive adequate summaries of the advisers' compliance program as part of a series trust structure. According to the SEC, the respondent, the fund administrator's compliance services affiliate, represented to the Board of Trustees that each adviser's compliance program was "sufficient and in use" and that the code of ethics and proxy voting policies were "compliant." The SEC charges that these summary representations did not satisfy Rule 38a-1(a)(2) which requires the board to make an initial determination that each fund service provider's policies and procedures are reasonably designed to comply with the securities laws. The SEC asserts that the respondent should have presented the Board with the advisers' compliance manuals or summaries of "the salient features of the advisers' compliance programs and that provided the Trustees sufficient understanding of how the programs addressed particularly significant risks." Separately, the SEC also took action against the fund directors for approving boilerplate Board minutes and shareholder disclosure that did not reflect the Board's activities when reviewing advisory contracts.

Compliance personnel for fund trusts with multiple advisers and sub-advisers should consider how to present the due diligence of the advisers' compliance programs. Delivering the full compliance manuals may avoid liability, but it may not help trustees in their decision-making process. Still open is how extensive a summary must be to qualify as adequate. Perhaps, compliance personnel should deliver both the summary and full manual. Regardless, this action increases liability for fund directors and fund service providers.

Fund Administrator Charged for Weak Compliance Procedures (*In re ALPS*; 7/2/15)

The SEC has charged a fund administrator that provided compliance services with causing violations of the auditor independence rules by failing to implement reasonable policies and procedures.[11] The SEC alleges that a director had an undisclosed consulting relationship with the fund auditor's affiliate. The SEC asserts that the fund administrator violated the compliance rule (38a-1) because it used D&O questionnaires that focused on the director independence rules rather than the auditor independence requirements and for failing to adequately train directors. The SEC also charged the auditor with improper professional conduct and the director for failing to disclose the relationship.

---

11   The administrator agreed to pay a $45,000 fine.

When a compliance violation occurs, the SEC will seek charges against all parties involved. This case applies a strict liability standard because it is unclear that training or a better D&O questionnaire would have disclosed the relationship between the director and the audit firm.

B. Valuation Firm. The SEC has asserted that a third-party valuation firm is an investment adviser.

SEC Deems Third Party Valuation Agent an "Investment Adviser" (*In re Six Financial and Beaumont*; 10/2/17)

A valuation firm was censured and fined and its principal was fined and barred for misleading its investment firm client about how it valued European options. The valuation firm represented that it valued the options using independent data and Black-Scholes modeling. The SEC charges that the firm merely used the estimated valuations provided by the client and then applied formulaic ranges. The SEC asserts that the valuation firm acted as an unregistered investment adviser because it "provided advice…about the value of securities…in exchange for compensation." Following therefrom, the SEC charged violations of Section 206(2) of the Advisers Act, which prohibits investment advisers form engaging in any fraudulent activity.

The SEC uses a tortured reading of the definition of "investment adviser" to hold accountable a third party valuation agent responsible for mis-pricing a fund. All service providers should beware that the SEC will seek to assert its authority through broad use of the securities laws.

C. Auditors. The SEC, through the PCAOB, supervises auditors and has brought cases for weak independence controls and rules violations.

Large Audit Firm Got Too Close with Its Clients (*In re Ernst & Young*; 9/20/16)

The SEC fined a large audit firm $9.3 Million and fined and barred engagement partners because close personal relationships compromised auditor independence for 2 separate public company engagements. In one case, the SEC asserts that the engagement partner spent over

$100,000 over a 3-year period to develop a close personal relationship with the issuer's CFO, including sharing vacation homes and going to football games. In the other case, the SEC alleges that the engagement partner maintained a romantic relationship with the issuer's Chief Accounting Officer. The SEC faults the firm for failing to probe how close personal relationships could compromise independence. The audit firm is charged with falsely asserting its independence in public filings and with violating auditing standards. The SEC's Director of Enforcement noted that these "are the first SEC enforcement actions for auditor independence failures due to close personal relationships between auditors and client personnel."

This line of reasoning could also have an impact on other securities markets gatekeepers such as administrators and lawyers. If a service provider becomes too close to its clients, can the SEC more easily assert an aiding and abetting charge if the client engages in wrongdoing?

Auditor Fined and Barred for Deficient Custody Audits (*In re Santos, Postal, & Co.*; 5/4/16)

An audit firm was fined and the engagement partner was fined and barred before practicing in front of the SEC for performing deficient custody audits. According to the SEC, the respondents issued clean custody reports even though one of the client's principals used his bill-paying authority to steal client funds. The SEC accuses the auditor of engaging in improper professional conduct by failing to (i) exercise due professional care and skepticism, (ii) obtain sufficient evidence and conduct adequate testing, (iii) prepare and maintain examination documentation, and (iv) assign an engagement team with "adequate training and proficiency" with the custody rule (206(4)-2). The SEC also charges the auditor with direct violations of the Advisers Act for filing misleading Forms ADV-E, the custody report required to be filed with the Commission.

The SEC expects gatekeepers to patrol the industry to weed out bad actors. Inexperienced professional services firms that wander into the investment management industry do so at their own risk. Ensuring compliance with the technical requirements of the Advisers Act is best left to auditors, lawyers, and compli-pros that specialize in this space. Neophytes will find themselves named on public enforcement actions.

Audit Partner and Manager Barred from SEC Work for Inflated Valuations (*In re Summit Asset Strategies et. al.*; 9/8/15)

An audit partner and manager were barred from appearing before the SEC for failing to follow professional standards in connection with the audit of a private fund. According to the SEC, the respondents failed to verify the existence of certain investments by confirming them with third parties and issued an audit report with inflated asset valuations. The SEC said that the auditors should have been on high alert because the previous auditor resigned over the same security. The adviser and its principal agreed to pay over $1.3 Million to settle the charges.

The SEC requires auditors to serve as securities markets gatekeepers. In this role, the SEC will hold the auditors accountable for ensuring that a fund has actually made purported investments. Also, the SEC suggests that the auditor also has a role in ensuring the proper valuation of illiquid investments.

D. Lawyers. The SEC has prosecuted outside lawyers for facilitating their clients' fraud.

SEC Names Securities Lawyer for Aiding/Abetting Hedge Fund Fraud (*SEC v. Shkreli et. al.*; 12/21/15)

The SEC charged a securities lawyer with aiding and abetting his hedge fund client's securities fraud.[12] The SEC alleges that the hedge fund manager lied to investors about performance and assets under management. The SEC asserts that he arranged sham consulting agreements between disgruntled hedge fund investors and a public company he controlled. In addition to charging the hedge fund manager with several violations of the securities laws, the SEC also charged his lawyer with aiding and abetting his violations of the antifraud rules. The SEC asserts that the lawyer drafted the sham consulting agreements and "knew or recklessly

---

12 He was subsequently convicted of conspiracy to commit wire and securities fraud, ordered to pay over $10 million in restitution, and sentenced to 18 months in prison.

disregarded that the true purpose of the consulting agreements was to settle potential claims." The SEC also faults the lawyer for failing to inform the company's Board.

The SEC's naming of a lawyer in an enforcement action breaks new ground in its prosecution of securities markets gatekeepers. In fact, we predicted such a case about a month ago. The SEC has indicated that securities markets service providers cannot simply take fees and ignore clients' misconduct.

Lawyer Barred for Failing to Conduct Adequate Due Diligence (*In re Lynch*; 4/11/17)

The SEC fined and barred an attorney from practicing before the Commission for failing to conduct proper due diligence as underwriter's counsel for misleading municipal bond offerings. According to the SEC, the lawyer prepared disclosure documents that contained erroneous statements that the issuer would comply, and had complied, with certain continuing disclosure obligations. The SEC faults the lawyer for failing to conduct proper due diligence and relying solely on statements from the issuer. The SEC also alleges that the lawyer ignored red flags that the disclosure was inaccurate. The SEC separately prosecuted the issuer and the underwriter.

We have previously predicted that the SEC would target lawyers as a class of gatekeepers responsible for policing securities markets. Counsel cannot ignore wrongdoing by claiming to have relied solely on client representations.

SEC Charges Lawyers for Clients' Securities Fraud (*In re Schneider and Wilson*; 10/17/17)

The SEC charged two lawyers with securities fraud for providing legal opinions and other assistance to fraudulent blank check company schemes. One of the lawyers also faces criminal charges brought by the U.S. Attorney's Office. The lawyers are accused of issuing due authorization and Rule 144 opinions, prerequisites to the public offering and sale of the shell companies, as well as other substantial assistance including moving assets through their lawyer trust accounts. The Director of the SEC's Miami Regional Office warned that "Lawyers are critical gatekeepers when it comes to protecting the integrity of our capital markets."

Lawyers and other securities markets gatekeepers cannot plead ignorance when red flags indicate that they knew or should have known about their clients' wrongdoing. Firms must conduct significant due diligence both before accepting a client and during representation. It is also noteworthy that the SEC charged the lawyers with securities fraud and not just aiding/abetting.

Lawyers Face Civil and Criminal Charges for Fronting Ponzi Scheme (*In re Flom and Schmidt*; 9/29/14)

Two Florida attorneys face civil and criminal charges for securities fraud for receiving funds on behalf of a Ponzi scheme.[13] The SEC alleges that the two attorneys served as a front to accept money from investors as part of a boiler room operation. The SEC claims the two lawyers kept 2% of the funds and transferred the remainder to the scheme's perpetrator, who misappropriated the funds. The SEC asserts that the attorneys' role "bolstered the appearance of safety in the investment opportunity and concealed from investors how the money was really being spent." Andrew M. Calamari, Director of the SEC's New York Regional Office, explained: "Attorneys are critical gatekeepers in our securities markets." The SEC charged the attorneys with securities fraud and aiding and abetting.

Lawyers and other industry providers should note that the regulator will hold them accountable for illegal actions by clients. It is unclear whether these industry gatekeepers will have direct securities law liability or aiding/abetting, which carries lesser penalties.

---

13   Both lawyers were subsequently convicted of criminal money laundering.

E. <u>Compliance Consultants</u>. Compliance consultants who fail to help their clients implement a reasonable compliance program will be held accountable.

Consultant Charged with Aiding/Abetting Compliance Breakdowns (*In re Parallax Investments*; 8/7/15)

A compliance consultant serving as his client's Chief Compliance Officer was censured, fined, and ordered to undergo 30 hours of training for aiding and abetting his client's failures to implement an adequate compliance program. The SEC also fined and censured the firm and its principal. The SEC cited a wide array of compliance breakdowns including (i) the failure to obtain client consent for principal transactions with an affiliated broker-dealer, (ii) a non-tailored "off-the-shelf" compliance manual, (iii) a lack of annual compliance reviews, (iv) no Code of Ethics enforcement, and (v) the failure to deliver financial statements for a private fund within 120 days as required by the custody rule (206(4)-2). The SEC charged the compliance consultant, a FINRA veteran with little SEC compliance experience, with aiding and abetting violations of the compliance rule (206(4)-7), the custody rule, and the prohibition on principal transactions without client consent (206(3)). The SEC noted that the compliance consultant spent less than 9 hours per month on the compliance program.

Not all compliance consultants are created equally. In this case, an allegedly unqualified consultant ignored the basic requirements of a reasonable compliance program, thereby contributing to the firm's noncompliance. This case also shows that consultants can be held liable for aiding and abetting their clients' violations.

SEC Alleges that CCO Failed to Verify AUM and Filed False ADV (*In re Aegis Capital et. al.*; 4/14/15)

The SEC has commenced enforcement proceedings against the Chief Compliance Officer of an investment adviser for failing to verify assets under management that he reported on Form ADV.[14] The SEC also filed

---

14   The CCO was fined and suspended from associating with an investment adviser or broker-dealer.

charges against the advisory firm, its Chief Operating Officer, and the CCO's consulting firm. The SEC faults the CCO for filing a Form ADV based on AUM obtained from the Chief Investment Officer whom the CCO "knew had little to no involvement with the Registrants' investment advisory accounts." According to the SEC, the CCO failed to "personally review" the adviser's records to verify AUM and the number of advisory accounts. The ADV reported AUM as $182 Million and 1200 client accounts, but the SEC alleges that the firm had only $62 Million in AUM and fewer than 300 clients. The SEC asserts that the CCO "collected the information from the CIO only hours before the filing deadline, and knew from the CIO's message that the information was only intended to be an estimate." The SEC also charges the firm with books and records violations for failing to segregate the adviser's financial records from its parent company.

A CCO should not blindly rely on information provided by firm management, especially if he/she has a reasonable belief that such information may not be reliable or accurate. Firms and CCOs must ensure a high level of compliance engagement that includes a robust testing program.

❑ The List: 10 Factors for Hiring a Compliance Consulting Firm

Many investment managers and boards struggle with the factors to consider when retaining a compliance consulting firm. They mistakenly assume that all compliance firms are the same. However, much like hiring any other professional service that seems inscrutable, compliance services firms can be analyzed by specific and objective characteristics. Below, we offer some guidance on how to evaluate a compliance consultant.

Ten Factors for Hiring a Compliance Consulting Firm

1.	**Size:** The sheer size of the firm makes a difference. A firm with more than 10 consultants will offer more knowledge, experience, depth, and services than a firm of 1-5 people.

2.	**Employee Experience:** Is the firm hiring senior professionals or newbies? Do they focus on former regulators or experienced business people? Is there a hiring philosophy that you can rely on, or are you just hiring the person in front of you rather than the firm? Employee turnover is a fact of life, so make sure you hire a firm that will offer consistency notwithstanding a particular employee.
3.	**Services:** Some firms offer holistic, ongoing services that may include providing a chief compliance officer. Some firms only provide mock audits. Inquire what the firm provides most of its clients. Also, ask about the testing program. How much time does the firm spend on testing activities? What does the report look like? Does the firm conduct interviews, review documents, engage in forensic testing, and sampling?
4.	**Clients:** Does the firm provide services to your industry? The investment management industry includes mutual fund managers, private equity firms, institutional money managers, family offices, and fintech companies. Does the compliance consultant have the relevant experience? How many clients does the firm serve?
5.	**SEC Exam Experience:** Don't assume that every compliance consultant has actually managed an SEC exam. Also, ask about results. Most reputable firms will not guarantee a perfect exam, but an experienced firm should be able to describe how it improved possible outcomes.
6.	**Service Model:** Compliance consulting is a professional service. Does the firm offer just one person or a team (which softens the impact of turnover)? Will they engage proactively without you calling first? Will they charge for every interaction (like a law firm)? How often will they come on-site?
7.	**Client Turnover:** This can be a red flag if a firm has experienced significant client turnover. It is always a good idea to ask to speak to a former client as well as a longstanding client.
8.	**Ownership:** Is the firm employee-owned or part of a large organization? Is there up-the-ladder accountability? Does the firm have other businesses (fund administration, accounting, brokerage) that could divert attention?
9.	**Tenure:** Firms that have been in business more than 5 or 10 years have a demonstrated track record that shows success and continuity. New consultants may be figuring out their business model, filling time between jobs, or auditioning for a job at your firm.
10.	**Insurance Coverage:** Shockingly, many compliance consultants do not carry E&O or professional liability coverage. We recommend a minimum of $1 Million in coverage.

F. __Underwriters.__ Underwriters also have disclosure obligations.

Underwriter Failed to Conduct Due Diligence (*In re O'Connor & Company*; 8/31/17)

A municipal underwriter was fined and censured, and its principal was suspended from the industry, for failing to conduct adequate due diligence. The public disclosure documents for the bond offerings at issue made misrepresentations about compliance with Continuing Disclosure Agreements. The SEC faults the underwriter for failing to conduct due diligence to determine the (in)accuracy of those misrepresentations, including its failure to check the Electronic Municipal Market Access website maintained by the MSRB. As a result, the underwriter violated several provisions of the securities laws by failing "to form a reasonable basis for believing in the truthfulness of the [issuer's] assertions that [it] had complied with its prior CDAs."

Market participants have an affirmative obligation to conduct due diligence on issuers and their disclosure statements. This obligation applies to underwriters, administrators, lawyers, consultants, and auditors, who, since the Madoff scandal, have found themselves in the regulatory cross-hairs as market watchdogs.

G. __Custodians.__ The SEC is reviewing how and for what services custodians charge clients.

Broker/Custodian Should Have Filed SARs to Report Advisers Act Violations (*SEC v. Charles Schwab*; 7/10/18)

A large custodian/clearing firm agreed to pay $2.8 Million to settle charges that it failed to file Suspicious Activity Reports about the conduct of dozens of terminated advisors that the SEC claims violated the Advisers Act. The SEC asserts that the Bank Secrecy Act required the custodian/clearing firm to file SARs when it suspected that advisers using its platform engaged in questionable fund transfers, charged excessive management fees, operated a cherry-picking scheme, or logged in as the client. According to the SEC, such unlawful activities fall within the SAR rules because they had no lawful business purpose or facilitated criminal activity.

The SEC is leveraging the Bank Secrecy Act, adopted to combat money laundering, to require broker/custodians to police advisers on their platforms for violations of the Advisers Act. It's a novel legal theory to further the regulator's enforcement goal of requiring large securities markets participants to serve in a gatekeeping role for the industry.

Custodian Charged with Securities Fraud (*SEC v. Alliance*; 8/14/14)

The SEC charged the Bahamas-based custodian of an asset manager charged with securities fraud with enabling the fraud and thereby violating the U.S. securities laws.[15] The SEC alleges that the custodian did not actually have custody of client assets because it wired the funds to the control of the asset manager. Additionally, the SEC avers that the asset manager created false account statements, which the custodian delivered to clients, prepared on the custodian's letterhead that the custodian provided. The SEC also asserts that the custodian was not independent because it shared office space with, and accepted an equity investment from, the asset manager. The SEC charges direct violations of the anti-fraud laws and rules as well as aiding and abetting.

This case will test the liability of a service provider to a defendant charged with securities fraud. Can a custodian (or other third party service providers) be held liable for direct violations of the anti-fraud rules when it did not sell securities? How far does aiding and abetting liability go? How does a service provider ensure that it conducts enough due diligence and maintains sufficient independence to avoid becoming entangled with a problem client?

Custody Bank Will Pay Over $380 Million to Settle FX Charges (*In re State Street*; 7/27/16)

A large custody bank agreed to pay over $382.4 million to settle charges that it misled clients about markups in FX transactions executed to

---

15   The custodian agreed to pay $337,000 in disgorgement of profits, and its principal agreed to pay a $50,000 fine.

settle trades. The total amount includes disgorgement and penalties to the SEC, the Department of Justice, and the Department of Labor related to plan clients. The amount does not include settlements with private plaintiffs in pending securities class action lawsuits. The SEC asserts that the respondent told mutual funds and other clients that they would receive competitive market rates, consistent with best execution, on FX trades, but then "set prices driven by predetermined, uniform markups and made no effort to obtain the best possible prices for these clients." The SEC charges violations of the Investment Company Act for delivering misleading confirmations and transaction reports.

When charging a client any fee or expense, assume that the regulators will retrospectively scrutinize the transaction. Always ensure full disclosure and consider foregoing the fee if disclosure cannot be made fully transparent.

FIVE ACTION ITEMS:

1. Enhance due diligence procedures before accepting a client.

2. Price in a risk premium for the inevitable bad actor.

3. Train employees on how to spot and report red flags.

4. Penalize sales personnel responsible for bad clients.

5. Only work with clients who work with other reputable service providers.

4

TREND

Flimsy compliance programs are scrutinized and punished.

The SEC adopted the compliance rule (Advisers Act Rule 206(4)-7 and Investment Company Act Rule 38a-1) back in 2004 after the mutual fund market timing scandal, which involved several fund firms allowing larger shareholders to market-time their funds to the detriment of smaller and longer-term investors. The SEC was initially caught flat-footed by then New York State Attorney General Elliott Spitzer, who used New York's broadly worded Martin Act to bring the first market timing cases. The SEC, playing defense with Congress and the public, argued that it needed similar authority to weed out wrongdoers alleged to have hurt shareholders with schemes not specifically prohibited by statute. The SEC pushed for a broadly worded compliance rule that applied to both advisers and mutual funds.

The market timing scandal allowed for the adoption of the compliance rule, but its real purpose was enforcement. As former Presidential Chief of Staff Rahm Emanuel (in)famously said, "You never want a serious crisis to go to waste." In fact, the SEC had wanted a compliance rule for many years before the market timing cases. Employing an argument that echoes today with the fiduciary standard (more on that later), the SEC wanted to implement a compliance requirement for advisers similar to the one already applicable to broker-dealers. The SEC could then bring an enforcement case against a firm for violating the compliance rule if it engaged in alleged wrongdoing that hurt clients or investors. The SEC rule would require advisers (and funds) to appoint a competent chief compliance officer who would be accountable for the compliance program, to adopt and implement policies and procedures, and to annually test those procedures

The compliance rule made the SEC enforcement job easier. Without the compliance rule, the SEC had to allege fraud or breach of fiduciary duty and prove some type of intent on the part of the defendant/respondent. The compliance rule avoids that problem by turning every allegation into a strict liability violation. When the SEC alleges a violation of the compliance rule, the client harm becomes the proof that the compliance policies and procedures were not sufficient; otherwise, the client would not have suffered harm. Poof! No more need to prove intent. Also, the compliance rule personalized liability (see above) by making the Chief Compliance Officer personally accountable to the SEC and liable for any firm wrongdoing. The SEC has often made statements about how CCOs really operate as deputized regulators.

The SEC waited a few years, but soon after the financial crisis, the Enforcement Division started bringing cases that alleged various compliance rule violations.

The first actions involved client harm and underlying violations where compliance failures were part of the pleadings. Over time, the SEC started bringing standalone actions for violating the compliance rule whether or not it could find client harm. As part of former Chairman Mary Jo White's "broken windows" enforcement campaign, the SEC argued that it must pursue technical violations of the compliance rule as a way to keep the "neighborhood" safe from bigger crimes that such firms would commit if allowed to continue down an unlawful path. The SEC brought cases alleging that CCOs were not qualified or committed, that policies and procedures were weak or "off-the-shelf," and that respondents failed to annually test the policies and procedures. Over time, the SEC brought even more technical cases as the definition of "reasonable" policies and testing expanded with the advent of the compliance profession.

Now that the compliance rule approaches its fifteenth birthday, a casual observer might assume that investment firms take the compliance rule seriously and understand the enforcement consequences of ignoring its requirements. While most firms know they have to implement a compliance program and appoint a Chief Compliance Officer, many investment advisers continue to resist substantive implementation. In February 2017, OCIE issued a Risk Alert to report that many firms had not implemented the basic requirements of an adequate compliance program. OCIE identified endemic industry problems such as "off-the-shelf" compliance manuals, weak testing, late filings, Code of Ethics deficiencies, and books and records retention failures. OCIE saw a large number of firms that violated the custody rule and the code of ethics requirements.

The SEC Enforcement Division, following up on leads from their OCIE colleagues, has brought a line of cases against advisers, broker-dealers, and their executives for widespread compliance failures. In *Trust & Investment Advisers*, the CEO and CFO were ordered to undergo mandatory compliance training and to hire a legitimate CCO after failing to address deficiencies raised during successive SEC exams. In *Barclay's*, a broker-dealer agreed to pay $18.8 million because it tried to jury-rig its broker-dealer procedures into an investment adviser manual but omitted several key topics, namely principal transactions, disclosures, marketing, custody, and books and records. In *Morgan Stanley*, the investment adviser agreed to pay a $13 million penalty because it failed to remedy a predecessor firm's compliance breakdowns. In *Dupree*, the SEC alleged that neither the firm nor its CCO—who also served as the firm's administrative assistant—were even aware that they were required to conduct an annual compliance review. In *du Pasquier & Co.*, the SEC faulted the firm for its template manual, best execution reviews, compliance personnel, disclosures, and code of ethics.

In a seminal corporate shakeup, the founder and CEO of Zenefits tendered his resignation because he fostered a corporate culture that ignored regulatory violations and internal controls. The Board, acknowledging the need to regain the confidence of customers and regulators, retained a CCO who had previously served as a federal prosecutor. Compliance had become necessary to achieve target revenue and profit goals. Zenefits and its CEO also agreed to pay nearly $1 million for failing to disclose compliance issues during fundraising.

The Enforcement Division has also begun to question whether firms have committed sufficient resources to compliance. In many of these cases, internal personnel were overwhelmed and pleaded for more resources before breakdowns that caused other violations or client harm. Based on our experience and industry studies, investment advisers should consider a benchmark of spending no less than 5 percent of revenue and/or 7 percent of operating budget on compliance costs, including personnel and technology.[16] Too little spent is a red flag that the firm does not take compliance seriously and, as a result, has a weak program. In *Pekin Singer Strauss*, the SEC faulted the firm because the CCO, who had limited compliance experience and spent less than 20 percent of his time on compliance, pleaded for more compliance resources, but his boss ignored him on the assumption that he would deal with issues after an exam occurred. In *Aviva*, the SEC maintained that the compliance officers were under-qualified, under-resourced, and under-trained despite requests made to upper management. In *LBMZ Securities*, the firm's CEO specifically said that he needed more revenue before he could spend on compliance.

The SEC is highly suspicious of the compliance "dual-hat" model whereby a senior executive with other primary responsibilities also acts as CCO. In most cases, such dual-hat executives do not have the time or the knowledge to properly serve in this function. In firms with a dual-hat CCO, the SEC has held executives accountable (with fines and/or bars) for dusty template manuals, a complete lack of compliance testing or reporting, insufficient disclosure, failure to address SEC deficiencies, and conflicts of interest. (See *In re Mohlman, In re Alison, and In re Coastal Equities.*)

---

16   This benchmark is not a rule, just a rule of thumb. Some firms may need to spend more; for example, emerging firms might spend up to 20 percent, and some firms may be able to justify less if the business is relatively uncomplicated and risk-avoiding.

Investment firms need more than a CCO and a compliance manual. They need to implement and test procedures. The SEC has become wise to what we call

> **"** The SEC has become wise to what we call "compliance alchemy," the practice of implementing a bogus compliance program that either furthers or fails to prevent regulatory misconduct. **"**

"compliance alchemy," the practice of implementing a bogus compliance program that either furthers or fails to prevent regulatory misconduct. For example, in *Deerfield Management*, a hedge fund firm had strict information barriers for expert networks but excluded "political research," a huge loophole that allowed traders to misuse material nonpublic information. There have been several analogous cases where broker-dealers failed to observe information barriers between research and trading (e.g. *In re Mizuho*).

Many firms have great compliance programs but fail to adequately monitor employees to ensure that the policies are followed. In *Deutsche Bank*, the large broker-dealer agreed to pay over $5 Million for failing to supervise its CMBS desk. In *Wells Fargo Advisers*, the firm took a $5 Million hit because one of its registered representatives engaged in insider trading. Faulty supervision has also led to significant fines for over-relying on automated surveillance tools (*In re Ameriprise*) and failure to supervise a corrupt CCO (*In re Budden*).

The SEC has also found weak compliance related to codes of ethics (*In re Federated Global Investment Management*), employee screening (*In re JP Morgan Securities*), and anti-money laundering (*In re Wells Fargo Advisors*).

After all these years and cases, and considering the availability of qualified lawyers and compliance consultants, registered advisers should be able to avoid compliance enforcement actions.

A. <u>Common Deficiencies.</u> OCIE published a list of the most common compliance deficiencies that included off-the-shelf compliance manuals, Code of Ethics problems, failures to follow procedures, and best execution.

SEC Publishes List of Most Cited Exam Deficiencies (2/9/17)

The SEC's Office of Compliance Inspections and Examinations has issued a Risk Alert listing the 5 most frequently identified compliance topics: weak compliance programs, insufficient and late filings, violations of the custody rule, Code of Ethics compliance deficiencies, and books and records. OCIE highlights specific compliance problems including untailored "off-the-shelf" manuals, weak or absent annual reviews, and failure to follow procedures. OCIE cited Form ADV and Form PF failures including inaccurate disclosures and late filings. Other common deficiencies include failures (i) to follow the custody rule due to lack of knowledge about its requirements, (ii) to identify access persons, and (iii) to maintain complete and accessible books and records.

Compliance with the Advisers Act is not intuitive. It requires a thorough knowledge of the specific requirements of the statute and all its rules. Firms must hire a regulatory professional or a compliance services firm to assist with compliance or face significant exam deficiencies or an enforcement action.

Advisers Failing Best Execution Compliance Obligations (7/16/18)

The SEC's Office of Compliance Inspections and Examinations (OCIE) issued a Risk Alert listing the most common deficiencies cited in recent examinations of advisers' best execution obligations. Reviewing over 1,500 exams, the OCIE staff highlighted advisers' failures to (i) conduct any best execution reviews, (ii) consider qualitative factors (e.g. execution capability, responsiveness), and (iii) utilize multiple brokers or to compare execution quality against other brokers. The OCIE staff also witnessed widespread failures to fully disclose best execution practices such as client preferences and soft dollar arrangements. The staff reports that many advisers either had inadequate policies and procedures or failed to follow them. The staff encourages advisers "to reflect upon their own practices, policies, and procedures in these areas and to promote improvements in adviser compliance programs."

In its recent fiduciary interpretation release, the SEC specifically identified best execution as core to an adviser's fiduciary obligation. As a core obligation, it concerns OCIE that they have identified pervasive compliance failures during examinations. Ensuring a best execution review should be part of every compliance testing program.

B. <u>Failing to Implement a Legitimate Compliance Program</u>. After more than a decade since the compliance rule's adoption, investment firms still fail to retain a chief compliance officer, implement tailored policies and procedures, or conduct annual reviews.

Founder/CEO Resigns over Compliance Failures (*Zenefits*; 2/22/16)

The founder and CEO of a large benefits consulting firm resigned over compliance failures. In a letter to employees, the new CEO said that the resignation resulted from inadequate internal compliance processes, controls, and actions. The new CEO also faulted the firm for a "culture and tone" that "have been inappropriate for a highly regulated company." He said that the revamped firm "has moved into a new phase of delivering at scale and needing to win the trust of customers, regulators, and other stakeholders." The firm also appointed a new Chief Compliance Officer, who previously served as a federal prosecutor, tasked with creating "best-in-class" compliance.

Failure to focus on compliance infrastructure can have the same negative consequences for senior executives as product failures, revenue shortfalls, or stock price declines.

RIA Execs Fined and Censured for Ignoring Compliance Program (*In re Trust & Investment Advisors*; 5/20/15)

The CEO and CFO of a registered investment adviser were fined, censured, and ordered to complete 30 hours of compliance training for failing to implement a reasonable compliance program. The firm was also ordered to retain an independent compliance consultant for 3 years. The SEC alleges that OCIE staff warned the firm, following 2005 and 2007 exams, that the firm lacked a compliance manual, failed to conduct annual compliance reviews, utilized misleading marketing materials that included performance information that did not show the effect of fees, and failed to retain a competent Chief Compliance Officer with knowledge in the Advisers Act. The SEC asserts that it found the same problems during a 2011 exam. The SEC charges violations of Section 206(4)-7 of the Advisers Act, which requires an

RIA to implement a compliance program to prevent violation so the securities laws.

Firms and their principals can and will incur regulatory liability for failing to implement an adequate compliance program even without allegations of underlying client harm. An adequate program must include a CCO with regulatory experience, a customized compliance manual, annual testing and reporting, and ongoing monitoring.

$15 Million Fine for Failing to Adopt Advisor Compliance Procedures (*In re Barclay's*; 9/25/14)

A large broker-dealer agreed to pay a $15 Million fine and reimburse clients another $3.8 Million for failing to adopt reasonable compliance policies and procedures after acquiring the investment advisory business of another large firm. The SEC asserts that the firm's compliance failings resulted in several violations of the Advisers Act. According to the SEC, the firm's compliance manual omitted advisor-specific provisions such as principal transactions, disclosure, marketing and solicitation arrangements, fee billing, custody, and books/records. The SEC charges the firm with several substantive violations including engaging in principal transactions without notifying clients, collecting undisclosed commissions on wrap fee programs, omitting disclosure about certain solicitation arrangements, and failing to include over 800 accounts in a custody audit.

Investment adviser compliance is not "BD Lite."[17] The Advisers Act's regulatory and compliance regime emanates from a fiduciary duty, which does not apply to BDs (yet). Broker-dealers that enter the investment advisory business through acquisition or otherwise must adopt specific compliance policies and procedures designed to ensure compliance with the Advisers Act. Merely relying on BD WSPs and the BD compliance personnel and infrastructure will leave serious gaps.

---

17 Very often, we hear broker-dealer compliance professionals make the incorrect assumptions that investment adviser compliance is the same as broker-dealer compliance without the formal FINRA requirements.

Compliance Failures Lead to Firm's Demise (*In re Aria Partners*; 8/27/18)

Compliance deficiencies led to the demise of a private fund manager because of failures to enforce a consistent redemption policy, deliver audited financial statements, and file accurate Form ADVs. According to the SEC, the firm allowed certain clients and insiders the ability to redeem before the stated 90-day redemption policy. The firm also failed to deliver audited financials as required by the custody rule. The SEC also cites the firm for filing inaccurate Form ADVs, including claiming SEC registration eligibility even though the firm had less than $100 Million in assets under management. The SEC attributes the failures to the firm's deficient compliance program which used a template manual and did not require annual compliance reviews.

 Failure to implement an adequate compliance program can have real-world implications for the viability of your firm. A tight compliance program will support a more coherent operating environment that will prevent sloppy business practices that will lose clients and attract regulators.

Adviser Agrees to Hire Experienced CCO to Settle Compliance Charges (*In re Moloney Securities*; 10/3/16)

The SEC fined and censured an investment adviser and its president/CIO for failing to implement compliance policies and procedures after the SEC noted principal transaction and best execution deficiencies during 2 separate exams. As part of the settlement, the respondent agreed to hire an experienced chief compliance officer and retain an independent compliance consultant. The SEC alleged that the respondent promised, but failed, to implement required principal transaction and best execution policies following SEC exams in 2006 and 2009. Even though the firm adopted policies and procedures, the SEC maintains that the firm violated those policies by continuing to engage in unlawful principal transactions and failing to monitor best execution.

 Investment firms must hire a competent, experienced, and fully-engaged chief compliance officer to maintain and implement the compliance policies and procedures. The SEC will not accept mere lip

*service when it comes to regulatory compliance, especially when a firm
does not follow through on specific undertakings made in response to
deficiency letters.*

RIA Failed to Conduct Annual Compliance Reviews and Appointed Admin as CCO (*In re Dupree Financial Group*; 10/6/16)

The SEC fined and censured a registered investment adviser for failing to
conduct annual compliance reviews and appointing a chief compliance
officer without relevant experience. The SEC asserts that the respondent,
which registered in 2010, never conducted an annual review of its
compliance policies and procedures as required by the compliance rule
(206(4)-7). In fact, according to the SEC, neither the firm nor the CCO
were even aware of the requirement. The SEC also faults the firm for
appointing as chief compliance officer an inexperienced administrative
assistant who spent most of her time on administrative duties.

*Compliance programs, at their most fundamental, must include
the implementation of effective policies and procedures reasonably
designed to achieve compliance with the Advisers Act, the appointment
of a qualified and dedicated chief compliance officer, and annual
reviews of the compliance program. The SEC will bring an enforcement
action for a weak compliance program even in the absence of any
other regulatory violation or client harm.*

SEC Prosecutes RIA for Weak Compliance Program (*In re du Pasquier & Co*; 1/23/15)

The SEC censured and fined a registered investment adviser because it
failed to implement an adequate compliance program as required by the
Advisers Act compliance rule (206(4)-7). The SEC cited several
violations: (i) using a template manual without tailoring it to the firm's
business; (ii) failing to conduct adequate best execution reviews; (iii)
designating compliance personnel that either did not devote sufficient
time to compliance and/or had insufficient knowledge and training; (iv)
failing to conduct adequate employee training; (v) filing incorrect ADVs;
(vi) not enforcing an adequate Code of Ethics; and (vii) failing to deliver
the Form ADV to clients.

❑ *The List: 10 Characteristics of an Effective Compliance Program*

What makes a good compliance program? It seems confusing when executive management listens to SEC speeches, interviews compliance professionals, or reads enforcement actions. Today's list provides the key characteristics that we examine when assessing a compliance program.

Ten Characteristics of an Effective Compliance Program

1.	**A qualified and dedicated Chief Compliance Officer:** The CCO should have significant (at least 5 years) Advisers Act regulatory knowledge and experience. Additionally, the CCO should be fully dedicated to the compliance function and not undertake other executive management roles.
2.	**Tailored policies and procedures:** The policies and procedures must be specifically tailored to the firm's business and continually reviewed and updated. An "off-the-shelf" manual is about as useful as internet-based medical advice.
3.	**Tone at the top:** How committed senior management is to compliance can be measured by 3 key variables: (1) total firm budget allocated to compliance (should be at least 5%); (2) executive time spent on compliance issues (at least quarterly); and (3) discipline for employees that violate compliance policies and procedures.
4.	**Training and communication:** A good compliance program must ensure that the entire organization has access to compliance information. Recommended practices include ongoing training and communication.
5.	**Testing and reporting:** A firm cannot have a good compliance program without requiring its people follow the rules. Firms must annually test all policies and procedures, record the findings and recommendations in a written report for management, and continually follow-up to ensure remediation.
6.	**Compliance calendar:** A good compliance calendar will serve as the working project plan of every activity required during the year. It should be written so that any new employee could follow the plan.

7.	**Books and records:** Documentation is the hallmark of a good compliance program. Only through well-maintained books and records can a firm log its compliance activities and demonstrate their effectiveness to senior management, clients, and the regulators. If it's not documented, it didn't happen.
8.	**Email review:** Very little transpires in an investment management firm without email communications. Email review can un-earth issues that annual testing may not. Email review adds "forensic" to testing.
9.	**Marketing materials:** An investment firm's marketing materials are its "canary in a coal mine" i.e. if the marketing materials are misleading or omit disclosures, very often the firm has deeper regulatory problems.
10.	**Outside advisers:** The best compliance programs use outside advisers to provide advice and an independent and best practices assessment. The regulatory world has become too complicated to go it alone.

C. Under-resourcing Compliance. Firms risk an enforcement action if they do not sufficiently resource the compliance function.

Adviser and its Principals Fined and Censured for Under-Funding Compliance (*In re Pekin Singer Strauss Asset Management*, 6/24/15)

An investment adviser and its principals were censured and fined a total of $285,000, and its President was barred from acting in a supervisory capacity, for failing to devote sufficient resources to the compliance program. According to the SEC, the President ignored consistent pleas from the firm's CCO for additional resources, including hiring a compliance consultant, and relief from his other responsibilities to implement an effective compliance program. Consequently, the SEC asserts, the firm failed to conduct annual compliance reviews and allowed multiple compliance violations to continue. These violations included Code of Ethics breaches and selling a higher-cost share class to clients. The CCO had little knowledge or experience in compliance or regulatory matters yet devoted less than 20% of his time to compliance matters because of his other responsibilities. The SEC said that the President chose to under-resource compliance activities and felt that he would deal with any issues if an exam occurred. As part of the settlement, the firm retained a CCO, another employee to help the CCO, an outside compliance consultant, and an outside securities lawyer.

Firms should devote no less than 5% of revenues on compliance infrastructure, which should include retaining a CCO (either internally or through a compliance services firm) that has knowledge and experience in compliance and regulatory matters. Compliance officers should note that the SEC did not take action against the CCO, presumably because he had identified the compliance weaknesses and pleaded for more resources.

Global Firm Gutted Valuation Control Function (*In re Citigroup Global Markets*; 8/17/18)

The SEC fined a large broker-dealer $5.75 Million for failing to allocate sufficient resources to its valuation control function, thereby allowing rogue traders to inflate securities valuations and positions. The firm eliminated 15 valuation control positions as part of a global efficiency initiative, which, according to the SEC, left the control function understaffed and under-trained to adequately implement the firm's valuation supervision policies. One manager complained internally that four staff members were tasked with verifying prices for more than 20 trading desks that held over $200 Billion in Level 2 and 3 securities. The SEC alleges violations of the books and records and supervision rules.

Having a valuation control function is not the same as having an effective valuation control function. Global firms must consider metrics before gutting compliance and supervisory functions that could ultimately allow bad actors to put the firm at risk. Firm leaders should think of compliance and supervision as the defense to protect assets and the firm's reputation. And, defense wins championships.

Under-Resourced Compliance Department Leads to Enforcement Action for Illegal Cross-Trading (*In re Aviva Investors*; 9/27/16)

The SEC fined and censured a fund manager because its under-resourced compliance department allowed unlawful cross-trading and principal trading. The SEC charges that the firm engaged in illegal cross-trading and principal trading between registered funds and other affiliated clients by using an interpositioned broker as part of pre-arranged transactions.

Although the firm had relevant written policies and procedures, according to the SEC, "the individuals working on cross trading within [the firm's] compliance department were underqualified, under resourced, and required additional training and resources to effectively implement [the] trading restrictions." The SEC faulted the firm, and not the compliance department, because "[s]enior members of the compliance department raised the need for additional compliance resources on multiple occasions to ... senior management" but those requests were not met. Much of the relevant monitoring was delegated to a "low-level administrative assistant" because of heavy compliance workloads.

The SEC will hold management accountable for failing to properly fund the compliance function, especially after the compliance department has informed management that more help is needed. As a guide, we recommend that firms spend no less than 5% of revenues or 7% of operating costs on compliance infrastructure, including personnel and technology.

Dual-Hatted CCO and Under-Resourced Compliance Function Result in Fine/Censure for BD (*In re LBMZ Securities*; 9/28/17)

The SEC fined and censured a broker-dealer because its under-resourced compliance function failed to implement adequate employee and information monitoring procedures. The firm's Chief Compliance Office, who also served as a relationship manager, was initially appointed despite a lack of compliance experience. He pleaded for more compliance resources, including the use of a third party compliance consultant, to monitor the firm's 45+ registered representatives, but the CEO refused because the firm "needed to generate more revenue before it could spend more money on compliance." As a result, the broker-dealer failed to review employee securities trading, review a sufficient number of emails, and monitor information barriers.

Registered advisers and broker-dealers should retain a fully-committed CCO – either through hiring or by retaining a third party compliance firm - that has significant compliance experience. Dual-hatting an unqualified internal employee will not satisfy the regulators. Also,

firms must adequately resource the compliance function. Based on previous benchmarking studies, most SEC-regulated entities spend between 7%-20% of total operating costs on compliance, with a minimum of 5% of revenues.

D. Dual-Hat CCOs. The SEC views a non-regulatory executive serving as a "dual-hatted" CCO as a compliance red flag.

Dual-Hat Principal/CCO Ignored SEC's Compliance Deficiencies (*SEC v. Mohlman*; 12/18/17)

The SEC has commenced enforcement proceedings against a fund manager and its principal/CCO for ignoring exam deficiencies about its compliance program and other violations. The SEC examined the respondents in 2010 and 2014 and noted several compliance deficiencies, which the SEC asserts the respondents ignored. The SEC charges the dual-hatted principal with failing to perform any work on the compliance program, adopting a stock manual that was not properly tailored to the business, or conducting any compliance review. The SEC also faults the respondents for charging compliance costs to the funds. The SEC additionally charges undisclosed conflicts of interest, misrepresentations, and valuation issues.

The SEC doesn't always give you a second chance to fix cited deficiencies. But when they do and you don't, expect an enforcement action. Also, this is another example of the failure of the dual-hatted CCO model, where an executive ignored his compliance responsibilities. Penny wise and pound foolish.

SEC Bars Dual-Hatted Executive for Inadequate Form ADV Disclosures (*In re Alison*; 4/4/17)

The SEC barred the principal/chief compliance officer of an investment adviser for inadequate ADV disclosure about revenue sharing and the firm's financial condition. The SEC also revoked the firm's registration. The SEC alleges that the firm's ADV failed to disclose that the principal received revenue sharing out of 12b-1 fees paid on client assets even though lower-expense share classes of the same funds were available. The SEC also faults the principal and the firm for failing to disclose its deteriorating financial condition including its difficulties meeting payroll and rent obligations. The SEC explained, "As the sole owner and chief compliance officer, it was [the respondent's] responsibility to review and ensure the accuracy" of Form ADV. The executive "should have known that the Forms ADV contained materially misleading statements and omitted material facts" but he "failed to exercise reasonable care in reviewing and signing" the ADV.

Advisers should have a dedicated chief compliance officer that knows the rules and can act as a check against conflicts of interest. The SEC has brought several enforcement cases against dual-hatted executives that short-change compliance.

IA/BD Failed to Supervise Its CEO/CCO (*In re Coastal Equities*; 12/12/17)

The SEC fined and censured an IA/BD for failing to supervise its CEO/CCO who was ultimately criminally convicted of stealing from clients. The CEO/CCO used the firm's consolidated reporting system, which allowed manual inputs of outside investments, as a way to mislead clients about false investments that he siphoned off into his own account. The SEC faults the firm for failing to implement reasonable policies and procedures to review the consolidated reports, which, according to the SEC, would have quickly uncovered the obvious scheme. The SEC charges violations of the antifraud rules and the compliance rule (206(4)-7), which requires firms to adopt and implement reasonable compliance policies procedures to prevent violations of the securities laws.

It's never good when the CEO (or any other revenue-producing individual) also serves as the CCO. Such a structure virtually ensures a lack of proper supervision. Firms must ensure that the CCO, whether inside or outsourced, has significant independence from management and the revenue-producing function. The SEC has brought several enforcement actions against dual-hatted CCOs, who also serve in a management capacity.

E. <u>Predecessor Compliance Liability</u>. A firm is responsible for compliance breakdowns at a predecessor firm that was acquired.

Large Adviser Fined $13 Million for Predecessors' Compliance Breakdowns (*In re Morgan Stanley Smith Barney*; 1/17/17)

A large investment adviser agreed to reimburse clients and pay a $13 Million penalty for compliance breakdowns related to fee billing, custody, and books and records. According to the SEC, over a 15-year-period, the respondent overbilled clients because of coding and administrative errors included in predecessor firms' billing systems. The SEC faults the firm for failing to test and uncover the over-billing when it integrated the systems. The SEC also accuses the respondent of violating the custody rule's surprise audit requirement by failing to properly identify the accounts subject to audit. Also, the SEC faults the firm's books and records practices for failing to retain client agreements. The SEC cites violations of the Advisers Act's custody rule (206(4)-2), compliance rule (206(4)-7), and books and records rule (204-2).

Integrating operations following a combination should trigger compliance due diligence into the prior firm's policies and procedures. Also, firms should include compliance due diligence as part of the acquisition process.

F. <u>Compliance Failures and 10b-5</u>. A firm must disclose compliance failures in fund-raising disclosure documents.

Private Company and CEO Misled Investors about Compliance Failures (*In re Zenefits*; 11/3/17)

A privately-held benefits consulting firm agreed to pay a $450,000 fine, and its former CEO agreed to pay over $500,000, for failing to disclose compliance failures during fundraising. The SEC maintains that the firm evaded state insurance licensing laws by rigging online examination courses and allowing employees to sell insurance without required licenses. The SEC charges that the firm violated the securities laws by failing to disclose the compliance failures when raising money from institutional investors during at least 3 financing rounds that raised over $500 Million. The related stock purchase agreements included false representations that the company complied with applicable laws including licensing requirements. The respondent has also faced regulatory actions by at least 40 states who have imposed more than $11 Million in sanctions. As part of the SEC settlement, the company created a Chief Compliance Officer position.

Be very careful when claiming compliance with applicable laws in disclosure or fundraising documents. You might want to ask your Chief Compliance Officer if any issues require more disclosure. The SEC can use holes in your regulatory compliance as a predicate to an enforcement action for securities fraud.

G. Bogus Compliance (aka "Compliance Alchemy"). The SEC will look beneath the appearance of a compliance program to investigate whether a firm actually implements effective policies and procedures. Just having policies and procedures and identifying a chief compliance officer won't satisfy your compliance obligations in areas such as information barriers, suspicious activity reports, cherry-picking, and employee screening.

1. Information barriers

Hedge Fund Traded on Inside Information from Political "Research Firm" (*In re Deerfield Management*; 8/23/17)

A hedge fund manager agreed to pay over $4.7 Million in disgorgement, interest, and penalties for failing to prevent trading on material nonpublic information received from a political research firm. Although the respondent had strict policies about information provided by expert networks, the firm's compliance policies had much lighter procedures for research firms, relying on employee self-monitoring and red flags. Nevertheless, the SEC asserts that the firm ignored red flags including the receipt of several pieces of material nonpublic information and the fact that the political intelligence analyst also served as the CCO. The SEC charges the firm with violating Section 204A of the Advisers Act, which requires the implementation of policies and procedures reasonably designed to prevent insider trading.

We call this "compliance alchemy" whereby a firm appears to write detailed compliance policies and procedures that allow behavior that the policies should be designed to prevent. In this case, there was no good reason to treat "research firms" different from "expert networks" when conducting insider trading due diligence.

Broker-Dealer Ignored Information Barriers for Issuer Share Repurchases (*In re Mizuho Securities*; 7/24/18)

The SEC fined a broker-dealer $1.25 Million for failing to respect required information barriers, thereby allowing the sharing of material nonpublic share buyback information with customers. The SEC alleges that the trading desk that executed issuer share repurchase trades shared order data with another desk that disclosed the information to customers. The head traders of the two desks shared trading intelligence including access to the order management system. The SEC maintains that the information was material to an investment decision because third party customers could use the trade orders as indications of the financial health of the underlying issuer. The SEC charges the firm with violating its own policies on information barriers.

It appears that the firm failed to implement a monitoring system to ensure that the trading desks observed information barriers. How firms ensure the protection of material nonpublic information should be part of the annual testing program.

2. Monitoring and supervision

Large BD Pays $5.3 Million to Settle Fail-to-Supervise Charges (*In re Deutsche Bank*; 2/15/18)

A large broker-dealer agreed to pay over $5.3 Million in remediation, disgorgement, fines, and interest to settle charges that it failed to properly supervise the traders and salespeople working on its non-agency CMBS desk. Additionally, the head of the CMBS desk was fired, fined, and suspended from the industry for failing to supervise. The SEC alleges that the CMBS desk regularly misrepresented terms and parties on the other side of secondary market CMBS transactions. Although the firm had policies and procedures and conducted training, the SEC faults the firm for not conducting "specialized training regarding the opaque CMBS secondary market" and for weak surveillance that "used generic price deviation thresholds in its trade surveillance to flag potentially suspicious trades instead of ones tailored to specific types of securities."

This case is an example of what we call "compliance alchemy" i.e. the appearance of a compliance program that does not actually discover or stop wrongdoing. Sure, the firm had policies and procedure prohibiting making misrepresentations. Sure, the firm provided compliance training. Yet, the compliance and surveillance team completely missed the ongoing scheme of misrepresentations on the CMBS desk.

Large IA/BD Fined $8 Million for Failing to Implement Suitability Procedures (*In re Morgan Stanley*; 2/16/17)

The SEC fined a large IA/BD $8 Million because it failed to implement compliance policies and procedures for the sale of single-inverse ETFs. Following warnings from FINRA and SEC OCIE staff, the respondent adopted policies and procedures requiring (i) every client to sign a Client Disclosure Notice and (ii) a supervisor to review all recommendations for suitability. However, over a 5-year period thereafter, the SEC maintains that 44% of clients did not sign a Disclosure Notice and most did not undergo adequate supervisory reviews. Consequently, the firm made several unsuitable recommendations including to retirement account clients. The SEC cites violations of the Adviser's Act's compliance rule (206(4)-7), which requires advisers to adopt and implement policies and procedures reasonably designed to ensure compliance with the Advisers Act.

The SEC will severely punish recidivists who were notified of deficiencies during a prior exam. In this case, the IA/BD specifically undertook to fix the identified suitability concerns but failed to implement those policies, thereby allowing the violative conduct to continue.

Large BD/IA Fined $5 Million for Failing to Detect Rep's Insider Trading (*In re Wells Fargo Advisors*; 9/24/14)

A large retail broker-dealer/adviser agreed to pay $5 Million to settle charges that its compliance policies and procedures were inadequate to detect and properly investigate insider trading by one of its 18,900 registered representatives. The SEC claims that the firm failed to follow up on red flags from several different functional areas, but the firm lacked the necessary coordination and internal communication. A group within the Compliance function investigated large positions in the subject security but closed the investigation with "no findings." The SEC also faulted the Compliance function for failing to follow procedures and ignoring required follow-ups.

This case shows the continuing trend by the regulators toward a strict liability standard for compliance breakdowns. This firm had policies and procedures which included testing. However, the firm missed detecting illegal conduct by one Rep among its nearly 19,000 registered representatives and advisory persons.

Over-Reliance on Automated Surveillance Tools Costs IA/BD $4.5 Million (*In re Ameriprise*; 8/16/18)

The SEC fined a large BD/IA $4.5 Million for overly relying on flawed compliance technologies that failed to prevent 5 registered representatives from stealing over $1 Million from clients over a 4-year period. One of the systems, which was designed to compare disbursement addresses against controlled addresses, contained a technical error that resulted in a failure to generate the necessary red flags for further investigation. The other system, a transaction-monitoring tool, had a design limitation that required an exact word-for-word address match, thereby failing to identify suspicious addresses. Complementary manual supervision and monitoring also failed to uncover the conduct. The SEC charges the firm with failures to supervise and to implement reasonable policies and procedures.

We love compliance regtech as a tool to leverage compli-pros' efforts to uncover wrongdoing. However, over-reliance on technology without professional judgment and intervention will lead to a false sense of

compliance security. An automatic hammer will not build a house without the architects and the builders.

Failure to Heed Compliance Consultant's Recommendations Results in Enforcement Action (*In re WFG Advisors*; 7/8/16)

The SEC fined and censured a wrap sponsor for double-charging clients on products in its wrap program even though a compliance consultant had twice warned the firm to change its practices. According to the SEC, the respondent told clients that it would not charge wrap fees if the client chose to pay commissions through an affiliated broker on purchases of certain BDC and REIT securities. The SEC asserts that the firm assessed over $34,000 in such fees over a 2-year period. Although the firm's compliance department was responsible for monitoring how fees were charged, the SEC, based on the compliance consultant's findings, alleges that the compliance function did not have sufficient human or technology resources to adequately monitor fee calculations.

Listen to your compliance consultant especially when the recommendation includes additional resources for a particular compliance weakness. Otherwise, the regulator will assume you lack the proper compliance "tone at the top" that regulators require.

Firm Principals Prosecuted for CCO's Wrongdoing (*In re Budden*; 4/28/16)

The SEC barred and fined the 2 principals of a registered investment adviser for failing to properly supervise the firm's Chief Compliance Officer, who was indicted for misappropriating client assets. The SEC asserts that the respondents "did nothing…to ensure that [the CCO] carried out his responsibilities" and "never provided any funding, training, or resources to support" the CCO. Specifically, the SEC alleges that the respondents failed to ensure (i) compliance with the custody rule by confirming that a surprise custody exam occurred, (ii) that the CCO implemented relevant policies and procedures, and (iii) that the firm performed annual compliance reviews. The SEC asserts violations of the compliance rule (206(4)-7), the custody rule (206(4)-2), and the supervision rule (203(e)(6)).

Firm principals do not absolve themselves of compliance responsibility by simply hiring a Chief Compliance Officer. They must continue to supervise the CCO to confirm proper implementation (and prevent wrongdoing) while also ensuring that the compliance function has sufficient resources and support.

3. Code of Ethics

Large Investment Manager to Pay $1.5 Million for Failing to Supervise Consultant (*In re Federated Global Investment Management*; 5/31/16)

The SEC censured and fined a large investment manager $1.5 Million for failing to subject to its Code of Ethics a third party consultant that was privy to material nonpublic information. The SEC charges that the consultant, who assisted the in-house portfolio management team with investment recommendations and company meetings, traded during blackout periods that would have been prohibited had he been deemed an "Access Person" under the Code. The consultant also served on the boards of companies in which the funds invested. The SEC faults the firm for failing to have a process to determine that the consultant should have been subject to the trading restrictions and reporting obligations of its Code of Ethics.

When considering the application of the Code of Ethics, the substantive duties matter more than the person's employment status. Our advice is to bring under the Code anybody who has information related to the investment process or portfolio holdings.

Investment Consultant Lied about Code of Ethics Compliance (*In re Slocum*; 2/10/17)

The SEC censured and fined an investment consultant and its principal $700,000 for lying about gifts received from recommended investment managers and performance information. The respondent's marketing material claimed that neither the firm nor its principals took "so much as a nickel" from any investment manager. However, the firm's Code of Ethics permitted gifts over $100 with pre-approval and under $100 without. The SEC asserts that personnel in the firm received tickets to the Masters Golf Tournament and other smaller gifts over a 4-year period, even where such gifts violated the Code of Ethics but the firm never imposed discipline. The SEC also accuses the firm of marketing hypothetical and back-tested performance without sufficient disclosure or backup.

Code of Ethics violations are an oft-cited SEC deficiency and should be remedied upon discovery (see Common OCIE Deficiencies). However, this firm compounded the problem by boasting about its Code of Ethics compliance in marketing materials. We do not recommend claiming 100% compliance with any rule as part of a marketing campaign.

4. Employee screening

Bank-Affiliated BD Fined $1.25 Million for Inadequate Employee Screening (*In re JP Morgan Securities*; 11/27/17)

FINRA fined a large bank-affiliated broker-dealer $1.25 Million for failing to conduct adequate background checks on over 8,000 associated persons over an 8-year period. The broker-dealer relied on its bank affiliate to conduct screening of its non-registered associated persons but the bank only screened for bank disqualifying criteria, not the broader categories of disqualification pursuant to Section 3(a)(39) of the Exchange Act and FINRA rules. Also, the firm completely failed to fingerprint over 2000 employees prior to employment. Four employees were retained despite statutory disqualifications. FINRA's EVP of Enforcement warned, "Firms have a clear responsibility to appropriately screen all employees for past criminal or regulatory events that can disqualify individuals from associating with member firms, even in a non-registered capacity."

FINRA has previously warned that it would review how firms screen for brokers with disciplinary records. The regulator wants to put pressure on the industry to drive out the bad brokers.

5. *Suspicious activity reporting and AML*

Bank to Pay $300 Million Penalty for Failing to Fulfill Compliance Commitments (*In re Standard Chartered Bank*; 8/20/14)

A large international bank agreed to pay a $300 Million penalty, cease lines of business, and appoint a special executive to settle regulatory allegations that it failed to implement proper anti-money laundering compliance procedures as part of 2012 settlement. An Independent Monitor, appointed as part of a 2012 settlement with the New York State Department of Financial Services, reported that the bank's AML compliance remediation efforts failed to detect a high number of high-risk transactions. The Monitor reported that the new compliance procedures were inadequate, and the bank failed to engage in adequate testing or auditing of the monitoring system. The bank agreed to appoint a "competent and responsible" executive who will report directly to the CEO to oversee the remediation.

Regulators will give no quarter when a firm fails to take the actions that it promised in a prior settlement.

Large BD Fined $3.5 Million for Curtailing SAR Filings (*In re Wells Fargo Advisors*; 11/14/17)

The SEC fined a large bank-affiliated broker-dealer $3.5 Million for failing to file anti-money laundering Suspicious Activity Reports (SARs). According to the SEC, the firm had an effective AML Surveillance and Investigations group, but new management attempted to reduce the number of filed SARs, investigations, and related record-keeping. During the 15 months under the new management, the number of SARs filed per month dropped 60%, from 57 to 22. The SEC charges that the respondent failed to file at least 50 required SARs during that period. An employee complaint triggered an internal investigation that uncovered the failures. Broker-dealers are required by the Bank Secrecy Act to file SARs to report transactions that the BD suspects involved funds derived from illegal transactions, had no apparent lawful business purpose, or used the BD to facilitate criminal activity.

Given the SEC's allegations that the broker-dealer's management intentionally tried to reduce SAR filings, the respondent and its management is fortunate that they do not face more severe civil or criminal penalties under the Bank Secrecy Act. There is no regulatory upside for choosing not to file SARs. When in doubt, file and avoid second-guessing by the regulators.

Resigning Compliance Head Blames Weak Centralized Compliance Function for AML Failures (*HSBC*; 7/18/12)

The Group Head of Compliance for a large international bank charged with failing to prevent money laundering blamed a weak centralized compliance structure for neglecting to implement adequate anti-money laundering procedures. The resigning official said that the group compliance function did not keep pace with the bank's rapid growth through acquisition, leaving too much autonomy to local affiliates and compliance personnel who did not report in to the corporate compliance group. He said that Group Compliance's mandate was to advise, recommend and report but lacked the authority, resources, support, and infrastructure to ensure that the affiliates followed policies and procedures. The new structure will properly resource the corporate compliance group and will require all compliance officers to report to a centralized function as well as separate the compliance function from the legal function.

This fight over resources and mission affects almost all compliance departments. Unfortunately, if a compliance failure occurs, blaming upper management for failing to deliver proper resources and support may not protect a compliance officer's job, reputation, or record.

Clearing Broker Charged with Failing to File SARs (*SEC v. Alpine Securities*; 6/7/17)

The SEC instituted enforcement proceedings against a clearing broker for failing to file required Suspicious Activity Reports as required by the Bank Secrecy Act. Although the broker-dealer had appropriate Written Supervisory Procedures, the firm failed in practice to implement its compliance program. The firm filed nearly 2000 SARs that omitted necessary descriptive information, failed to file follow-up SARs with respect to another 1900 transactions, and did not file 250 SARs within the required time frames. The SEC claims that the deficient SARs "facilitated illicit actors' evasion of scrutiny by U.S. regulators and law enforcement."

The BSA is no joke. Failure to file SARs can result in crippling fines (up to $25,000 per failed SAR) and land you in jail. It should be Chapter 1 of a broker-dealer's compliance program.

Compliance Officer Failed to File Suspicious Activity Reports (*In re Terracciano*; 7/13/18)

A compliance officer was fined, and faces further action, for failing to file Suspicious Activity Reports. The SEC asserts that the respondent observed significant red flags indicating illegal activity including high trading volume in companies with little business activity. He also received alerts about suspicious trading activity from the clearing firm. The SEC faults the respondent for ignoring his own Written Supervisory Procedures by failing to file reports, investigate suspicious trading, or produce a written analysis demonstrating that he had considered filing SARs. His firm was previously censured and fined.

The Treasury Department's Financial Crimes Enforcement Network (FinCEN) maintains that a compliance officer is liable for up to $25,000 for every SAR not filed. It's not enough to have policies and procedures. A compliance officer must implement those procedures and monitor and address potential violations.

6. Branch Offices

SEC Reviewing Multi-Branch Adviser Compliance (1/3/17)

The staff of the SEC's Office of Compliance Inspections and Examinations issued a Risk Alert announcing its "Multi-Branch Adviser Initiative." The Alert expresses concern about the "unique risks and challenges" for advisers operating through branch offices geographically separate from the principal place of business. The Initiative will focus on compliance program elements including the supervision structure, the role and empowerment of compliance personnel, and implementation of policies and procedures. The staff will also review investment recommendation oversight, conflicts of interest, and allocation of investment opportunities. The OCIE staff will assess how multi-branch firms exercise oversight and supervision of branch office activities.

The SEC is catching up with FINRA, which has longstanding prescribed oversight obligations for OSJs and branches. For compliance officers, oversight of far-flung operations creates additional information and supervision challenges that often exceed current resources.

FIVE ACTION ITEMS:

1. If you can't afford a full-time internal CCO, retain a compliance outsourcing firm that can provide a qualified CCO.

2. Review your compliance spending budget to ensure that you are spending at least 5 percent of your revenues on compliance.

3. If you engage a mock audit, make sure you address all of the recommendations within six months.

4. Implement automated surveillance tools to the extent available and affordable, especially in areas such as personal trading, best execution, and portfolio compliance.

5. Don't use the compliance program as a bureaucratic tool. If your compliance program facilitates wrongdoing rather than stops it, you should rethink your risk management priorities.

TREND 5

A super-fiduciary standard is challenging investment advisers.

To fiduciary or not to fiduciary—that is the question. Although the debate rages over a fiduciary standard for brokers, investment advisers have been subject to a fiduciary standard since 1940. Over the last several years, however, the SEC has become increasingly ardent in enforcing the fiduciary standard and has raised conduct standards through an alarming number of enforcement actions. In April 2018, the SEC made this super-fiduciary standard more explicit when it issued an interpretation that raises the conduct bar for an adviser's duty of care, duty of loyalty, best execution obligations, and client monitoring responsibilities. OCIE followed up with a laundry list of best execution problems. The states and private organizations have also adopted or proposed a broader fiduciary standard of care.

> **[The SEC Enforcement Division] will allege a breach of fiduciary duty anytime it sees an adviser capitalizing on its position of trust with its clients in a way that benefits the adviser.**

Over the years, the SEC Enforcement Division has used breach of fiduciary duty as its main litigation weapon because it can cover a broad range of alleged misdeeds. It will allege a breach of fiduciary duty anytime it sees an adviser capitalizing on the adviser's position of trust with clients in a way that benefits the adviser.

When considering an adviser's fiduciary duty, the SEC has expressed significant concern about how advisers recommend securities, with a particular focus on mutual fund share classes. In 2016, OCIE launched its Share Class Initiative, an industry sweep of compensation arrangements related to mutual fund share classes. Enforcement actions predictably followed. In *Katz*, the adviser paid over $2 Million to settle best execution charges for recommending share classes that paid back 12b-1 fees. In *SunTrust Advisory Services*, the SEC faulted the respondent for failing to move clients to lower-fee share classes as they became available. The SEC did not believe the adviser's conflicts of interest disclosure fully described its financial interest in receiving revenue sharing from the underlying funds.

Seeing a broader pattern of wrongdoing, the SEC began to investigate wrap programs—a product that was supposed to avoid conflicts of interest because the client pays an all-in asset-based fee for advice and brokerage regardless of the underlying securities or funds selected. Years ago, many broker-dealers created wrap programs so that regulators couldn't accuse them of churning—the practice of rapid trading for the sole purpose of earning commissions. Ironically, in *Royal Alliance*, the SEC accused the adviser of reverse churning, *i.e.,* charging the client an ongoing asset-based fee that generated more revenue for the firm than a traditional brokerage account because the client wrap accounts traded so infrequently. The SEC has also charged wrap sponsors with failure to conduct the promised due diligence on underlying funds (*In re Barclay's Capital*) and for failing to prevent underlying advisers from trading away from the broker whose charges were included in the wrap fee (*In re RW Baird & Raymond James; In re Lockwood*).

Not content to focus solely on the receipt of compensation, the SEC has also criticized advisers for paying solicitors who could deliver public plan assets for management. Following a 2010 pay-to-play scandal involving New York State retirement assets, the SEC adopted Rule 206(4)-5, which prohibits firms from receiving asset management compensation if they contribute, directly or indirectly, to local and state political campaigns for elected officials that could direct investment mandates. The SEC fined one large investment bank $12 Million because it allowed a senior employee to leverage firm resources to support the campaign of the Massachusetts Treasurer (*In re Goldman Sachs*). The SEC has also brought cases against private equity firms (*In re TL Ventures*) and several wealth management firms for direct violations of the rule (*In re NGN Capital et al.*).

The OCIE and Enforcement staffs continue to examine other areas of fiduciary interest. For example, firms still try to cherry-pick trades for the benefit of proprietary accounts or favored clients by using omnibus trading accounts (*SEC v. Strategic Capital Management; SEC v. Breton*). When firms recommend proprietary products, the SEC raises fiduciary red flags about disclosure and self-dealing (*In re JP Morgan*). The Enforcement Division also continues to bring fiduciary charges for a wide variety of misdeeds, including violating investment limitations (*In re Balter*), misappropriating client funds (*SEC v. Rogicki*), and lying to clients (*SEC v. Drake*).

A. <u>New Conduct Standard for Advisers</u>. The SEC proposed a reinterpreted fiduciary conduct standard for advisers that creates a super-fiduciary duty.

SEC Proposes Broker Best Interest Standard (4/19/18)

The SEC has voted to propose a best interest standard for broker-dealers giving advice to retail customers, defined as persons who use the recommendation primarily for personal, family, or household purposes. The proposed "Regulation Best Interest" requires a broker to act in the best interest of the retail customer at the time the recommendation is made, notwithstanding their own financial interests. The broker must disclose its conflicts of interest and have a reasonable basis to believe the recommendation and the series of transactions are in the client's best interest. The proposal also requires that brokers and advisers deliver a new disclosure form describing the relationship and conflicts of interest. The rule defers to existing broker-dealer regulations in defining the term "recommendation." The SEC has also proposed a companion rule seeking to clarify an investment adviser's fiduciary duty, including the obligation to provide advice in the best interest of the client, the duty of best execution, the commitment to provide ongoing monitoring, and the duty of loyalty.

Don't change anything yet based on this proposal. Expect much debate during the comment period and thereafter, as even one of the SEC commissioners has dissented. Our view is that brokers should be subject to the same fiduciary standard as investment advisers. We don't understand why the SEC would take this half-measure and enhance the broker standard without making it the same as the adviser standard. This confusion is bad for customers and for brokers.

Advisers Failing Best Execution Compliance Obligations (7/16/18)

The SEC's Office of Compliance Inspections and Examinations (OCIE) issued a Risk Alert listing the most common deficiencies cited in recent examinations of advisers' best execution obligations. Reviewing over 1,500 exams, the OCIE staff highlighted advisers' failures to (i) conduct any best execution reviews, (ii) consider qualitative factors (e.g. execution capability, responsiveness), and (iii) utilize multiple brokers or to compare execution quality against other brokers. The OCIE staff also witnessed widespread failures to fully disclose best execution practices such as client preferences and soft dollar arrangements. The staff reports that many advisers either had inadequate policies and procedures or failed to follow them. The staff encourages advisers "to reflect upon their own practices, policies, and procedures in these areas and to promote improvements in adviser compliance programs."

In its recent fiduciary interpretation release, the SEC specifically identified best execution as core to an adviser's fiduciary obligation. As a core obligation, it concerns OCIE that they have identified pervasive compliance failures during examinations. Ensuring a best execution review should be part of every compliance testing program.

Massachusetts Sues to Enforce Compliance with Fiduciary Rule (*In re Scottrade*; 2/16/18)

The Massachusetts Securities Division has commenced administrative proceedings against a large broker-dealer because it ran sales contests that violated its own policies adopted to comply with the Department of Labor's fiduciary rule.[18] The DoL rule, which became effective in June 2017, requires firms to follow an "impartial conduct standard" including acting in the best interest of customers, charging reasonable compensation, and ensuring full disclosure. In response to the rule, the BD adopted compliance policies prohibiting conflicts of interest when dealing with retirement accounts. Following adoption of the new policies, the firm launched sales contests, which the MSD alleges involved misrepresentations and conflicts of interest. The MSD alleges that the firm violated Massachusetts ethical conduct standards by failing to abide by its own policies and the DoL rule.

Even though he DoL won't enforce the fiduciary rule, the impartial conduct standard applies to firms that recommend products to retirement accounts. Nevada has already passed its own fiduciary legislation. Now, Massachusetts uses its enforcement powers to compel fiduciary compliance. Expect other states to follow.

---

18   The future of this case is unclear now that the rule has been vacated.

CFP Board Proposes Fiduciary Standard (6/21/17)

The CFP Board has proposed a broad fiduciary standard in its new Code of Ethics and Standards of Conduct. The proposed fiduciary standard requires a CFP professional to exercise a duty of loyalty, which requires placing the client's interests above those of the CFP or his/her firm, avoiding or fully disclosing conflicts of interest, and acting without regard to personal or firm financial interests. The new Code requires disclosure of all conflicts of interest such that a client can provide informed consent. Comments on the proposed Code are due on August 21.

 Whether or not the DoL or the SEC moves ahead with a fiduciary standard, the CFP Code would apply a best interest standard to many of the high-end planners carrying the CFP designation. The fiduciary genie appears to be out of the lamp.

❑ *The List: Ten Prohibited Conflicts of Interest*

The SEC often alleges "conflicts of interest" in various enforcement actions and also derides "conflicts" in letters, speeches, testimony, and other public statements. In order to help clarify what the SEC means by "conflict of interest," today's list describes ten prohibited practices that the regulators have identified as conflicts of interest in enforcement cases.

Tem Prohibited Conflicts of Interest

1.	**Recommending the wrong share class:** The SEC has brought several cases where wrap or managed account sponsors recommended share classes that were not the lowest cost available. In many cases, the SEC alleged a conflict because the respondent received some sort of financial benefit, such as loads or revenue sharing.
2.	**Recommending proprietary products:** The regulators highly scrutinize advisers and broker-dealers who recommend proprietary funds or managed account programs that include built-in fees.
3.	**Favoring certain clients:** The SEC has criticized firms for allowing redemptions to favored clients after telling other clients a fund was closed to redemptions or by selling out liquid investments for insiders and leaving outside clients holding illiquid investments.

4.	**Manipulating valuations to increase fees:** Firms have tried all manners of schemes including using "friendly" broker quotes, lying about inputs, and using noneconomic options trades.
5.	**Making sweetheart deals with affiliates:** The SEC will not like firms who feign "independence" and then recommend affiliates for ancillary services to jack up revenue.
6.	**Cherry-picking allocations:** Several firms have been prosecuted for using omnibus accounts and then retroactively cherry-picking good trades for proprietary accounts and assigning not-as-good trades to client accounts.
7.	**Taking undisclosed fees:** The fee may appear legitimate (and maybe the client should have known), but, without specific written disclosure, a firm looks like it has engaged in a classic conflict of interest when it surreptitiously takes undisclosed compensation. Examples include payment of overhead expenses, consulting fees, and investment banking fees.
8.	**Overbilling clients:** Firms have found regulatory trouble by overbilling clients by using an opaque billing formula, such as changing measurement dates for valuing client assets or failing to deduct unrealized losses.
9.	**Lying about performance or strategy:** The SEC views misleading marketing materials as a form of conflict of interest. There have been many criticized practices including using backtested data, failing to describe a strategy's true risks, omitting poor recommendations from performance calculations, and cherry-picking time periods.
10.	**Lying about qualifications:** In addition to performance, the SEC has also faulted firms who lie about their academic or business qualifications, the firm's AUM, or the firm's financial or disciplinary record.]

B. Lowest Cost Mutual Fund Share Classes. The SEC has brought several cases alleging that advisers failed to offer the lowest cost mutual fund share class available or failed to offer sales charge waivers.

OCIE Launches Share Class Initiative (7/14/16)

The SEC's Office of Compliance Inspections and Examinations has issued a Risk Alert announcing its Share Class Initiative, which will examine how advisers recommend mutual fund and 529 share classes. The Risk Alert indicates that the exam staff will review whether an adviser has satisfied its fiduciary duty and best execution obligations when recommending a more expensive share class when a less expensive share class of the same fund is available. OCIE will also scrutinize load and distribution compensation received through affiliates and whether such compensation arrangements are properly disclosed in Form ADV Part 2. Also, the exam staff will review relevant compliance policies and procedures concerning the share class selection and recommendation process. In the Risk Alert, OCIE "encourages advisers to reflect upon their own practices, policies, and procedures in these areas and to make improvements in their advisory compliance programs where necessary."

Compli-pros should review any recommendations of share classes that carry a load or distribution fee (including 12b-1 or shareholder servicing fee). An adviser who recommends such share classes will have the burden of defending why it didn't recommend a less expensive share class.

Large BD/IA Pays $2.2 Million for Recommending Wrong Mutual Fund Share Class (*In re Ameriprise*; 3/2/18)

A large BD/IA agreed to pay $2.2 Million in remediation, interest and penalties for failing to recommend the lowest mutual fund share class available to retirement plan customers. Instead of recommending load-waived "A" shares, the respondent recommended other higher-cost share classes that resulted in compensation paid to the BD/IA. The SEC faults the firm for failing to have adequate systems and controls in place to ensure that retirement clients benefitted from available discounts. The SEC also asserts that the BD/IA omitted necessary disclosures about revenue sharing and the impact on overall investment returns. An SEC Enforcement official warned that "these types of actions remains a priority for the Division" as evidenced by its recently-announced Share Class Selection Disclosure Initiative.

Firms must implement a system to ensure that eligible clients get the waivers to which they are entitled. Compliance can't rely on reps self-policing, especially when they receive higher compensation on certain share classes.

Adviser Failed Best Execution When Recommending 12b-1 Fund Class (*In re Katz*; 4/5/17)

An investment adviser agreed to pay over $2 Million in disgorgement, interest and penalties for failing to buy the least expensive share class of recommended mutual funds. The SEC maintains that the respondent, an investment adviser representative of a large advisory firm, recommended Class A shares that carried a 12b-1 fee instead of lower-expense institutional shares. The adviser received a portion of the 12b-1 fees from the clearing firm as revenue sharing. The SEC did not absolve the adviser even though he received approval for the practice after consulting his firm's management. The SEC asserts that the adviser violated his obligation to seek best execution for securities transactions.

The SEC requires advisers to recommend the lowest-expense share class available, which requires more diligence by advisers before making recommendations. It is also noteworthy that the SEC uses an expansive interpretation of an adviser's best execution obligations, which historically has centered on brokerage commissions.

Wrap Sponsor Failed to Update Compliance Policies for Lower Share Classes (*In re SunTrust Investment Services*; 9/20/17)

The IA/BD subsidiary of a large bank agreed to pay almost $1.3 Million in disgorgement and a $1.1 million fine for putting wrap fee clients in funds that paid a 12b-1 fee back to the selling reps. The SEC faults the firm for failing to recommend that clients move assets into lower-fee share classes as those classes became available over time. Although the firm disclosed that it may receive 12b-1 fees, it did not disclose that it actually received those fees and that lower classes were available. The SEC noted that the IA/BD made changes to qualified accounts but failed to implement similar changes to non-qualified accounts. In addition to best execution, fiduciary, and disclosure violations, the SEC criticized the firm's compliance program because the respondent failed to update its compliance policies and procedures as institutional share classes became available.

A compliance program is not a static exercise that you can set and forget. As the markets and the business changes, firms must continuously review policies and procedures to determine if they still make sense given new realities. In this case, the wider availability of institutional share classes necessitated changes to the firm's compliance practices.

C. <u>Wrap Programs.</u> The SEC has scrutinized wrap programs for due diligence, share classes, trading away, billing, and reverse churning.

Wrap Sponsors to Pay over $9.5 Million to Settle Share Class and Reverse Churning Charges (*In re Royal Alliance et al*; 3/17/16)

Three related dually registered adviser/BDs agreed to pay a $7.5 Million fine and pay another $2+ Million in disgorgement and penalties for violations related to their wrap programs. The SEC charges the firms for recommending mutual fund share classes that paid 12b-1 fees to the firms when other share classes were available. Although the respondents' Form ADVs included disclosure that they would receive 12b-1 fees from recommended products, the SEC faults the firms for not disclosing that they would not recommend the lowest share class available. The SEC also charges the firm with violations of the compliance rule (206(4)-7) for failing to follow their own policies and procedures requiring account reviews to protect against reverse churning (i.e. wrap fee clients that would be better suited in a traditional brokerage account because of low transaction volume). The SEC indicates that it "has been actively probing conflicts of interest and disclosure around mutual fund share class selection."

We believe the SEC is implicitly outlawing revenue sharing with advisers, unless an adviser can shoulder the compliance burden of proof that the client could not have done better in the absence of the payments to the adviser. Here, the firm did in fact disclose that it would receive payments from underlying products, yet the SEC still found fault because the firm could have found lower fee share classes, which presumably would have precluded revenue sharing. The reverse churning charges make it difficult for dually-registered advisers to efficiently operate a wrap program without significant ongoing compliance oversight.

Wrap Sponsor Pays $97 Million for Inadequate Due Diligence (*In re Barclay's Capital*; 5/11/17)

A large bank agreed to pay $97 Million, including a $30 Million fine, for compliance failures in its wrap programs. The bank represented in marketing materials and Form ADV that it performed significant initial and ongoing manager due diligence. However, according to the SEC, during a 5-year period from 2010 to 2015 (when it sold its wrap business), the respondent failed to perform such due diligence on several programs and managers because of a lack of internal resources and miscommunications between functions, even though the bank continued to charge significant account level fees to provide such services. The respondent was also charged with overbilling clients as well as using more expensive mutual fund share classes when lower-fee classes were available. As part of the settlement, the bank agreed to pay $3.5 million in customer remediation and $49.7 Million in fee disgorgement in addition to interest and the fine.

Over the last 2 years, the SEC has warned about wrap programs (See e.g. SEC 2017 Exam Priorities Letter) and has brought several cases against wrap sponsors alleging a number of violations: trading away, reverse churning, revenue sharing, mutual fund share classes. In this case, the SEC adds a requirement that the fees charged must be commensurate with the due diligence services provided. This analysis appears borrowed from mutual funds where Boards must ensure the reasonability of fees charged. We recommend that compli-pros perform an internal sweep of wrap practices before the SEC shows up at the front door.

Wrap Sponsors Fined for Failing to Disclose Trading Away Commissions (*In re RW Baird and Raymond James*; 9/9/16)

The SEC fined two wrap program sponsors $600,000 and $300,000, respectively, for failing to adequately disclose trading away commissions. The SEC acknowledges that both firms did disclose that program sub-advisers could use non-program brokers to obtain best execution and that these trading away commissions would increase client costs. However, the SEC faults the respondents for failing to analyze or detail these costs because they were embedded in securities prices when reported to clients. The SEC asserts that the wrap sponsors violated the compliance rule (206(4)-7) by failing to implement policies and procedures necessary to ensure suitability and informed client consent. The SEC said it will continue to assess wrap programs and "whether advisers are fulfilling fiduciary and contractual obligations to clients and properly managing such aspects as disclosures, conflicts of interest, best execution, and trading away from the sponsor broker-dealer."

The SEC continues its assault on wrap programs, criticizing disclosures, brokerage commissions and investment selections. We are not sure any amount of disclosure will pass muster, but wrap sponsors should consider a regulatory reexamination of their programs.

Large Wrap Sponsor Pays $18.3 Million for Compliance Problems in Business Sold 8 Years Ago (*In re Citigroup Global Markets*; 1/30/17)

A large dually registered adviser/broker-dealer agreed to pay over $18 Million to settle charges that it overbilled clients in a wrap program that it sold off in 2009, although it maintained an interest through 2013. The SEC charges that the respondent overbilled clients by failing to (i) input lower negotiated fees into its system, (ii) track transferred accounts, (iii) rebate prepaid fees after termination; (iv) benefit investors when rounding, and (v) track lower rates when switching platforms. The SEC faults the firm for failing to implement adequate compliance policies and procedures (Rule 206(4)-7) that would have required sample testing to discover the over-billing. The SEC also charges violations of the books and records rule (204-2) because the respondent could not locate over 83,000 advisory contracts.

Selling or terminating a business line does not cut off regulatory liability for prior events. Also, this case is a good example of how overbilling could occur and how to test for irregularities.

D. Pay-to-Play. The SEC will question firms that pay solicitors to obtain public plan business.

SEC Fines 10 Firms for Violating Anti-Pay-to-Play Rule (*In re NGN Capital et al*; 1/18/17)

The SEC fined 10 advisory firms over $650,000, ranging from $30,000 to $100,000, for accepting compensation to manage city or state pension funds within 2 years of a disqualifying campaign contribution. The SEC alleges that the firms violated the anti-pay-to-play rule (206(4)-5) by failing to observe the 2-year timeout after a designated covered associate makes a campaign contribution to a candidate who could influence manager selection. An SEC official explained, "The two-year timeout is intended to discourage pay-to-play practices in the investment of public money, including public pension funds."

The anti-pay-to-play rule is strict liability i.e. the SEC does not need to show that the campaign contribution actually resulted or contributed to the decision to grant the mandate.

Fund Managers Fined for Disqualifying Political Contributions (*In re Sofinova Ventures, Encap Investments, and Oaktree Capital Management*; 7/11/18)

The SEC fined an investment adviser and two exempt reporting advisers for violating the pay-to-play rule (206(4)-5) that prohibits accepting adviser compensation during the two-year period following a political contribution to an official that could influence the awarding of investment mandates. In all three cases, one or more public plans had significant investments in funds managed by the respondents before the disqualifying campaign contributions. The campaigns included those for governor, state attorney general, state treasurer, and Superintendent of Public Instruction.

The pay-to-play rule is a strict liability rule. It doesn't matter if contributions were returned, investments preceded the contributions, the government entity invested in a fund, or there was no intent to influence a mandate. Also, exempt reporting advisers should note that they are also subject to the pay-to-play rule. The only real remedy once a firm discovers that a disqualifying contribution was made is to forego fees on the investment for two years. To avoid the compliance monitoring headaches, we recommend that firms prohibit their employees from making political contributions.

Investment Bank to Pay $12 Million for Pay-to-Play Violations (*In re Goldman Sachs*; 10/1/12)

A large investment bank agreed to pay nearly $12 Million in disgorgement, interest, and penalties for violating the pay-to-play prohibitions when a senior banker worked for a gubernatorial campaign. The SEC alleges that the banker used firm resources and operated during work hours to assist the Massachusetts Treasurer's campaign for governor. The SEC charges that his campaign activities constituted "in-kind" campaign contributions which required the firm to refrain from any municipal underwriting business in Massachusetts for two years. The SEC also charged the firm for failing to supervise because, although the firm knew of his political activities, the only supervision included a certification by the banker and general e-mail reviews. The firm was charged with violations of MSRB Rule G-37, which is the model for Rule 206(4)-5 under the Advisers Act. The SEC has also commenced enforcement proceedings against the banker.

Firms should note the following from this case: (a) in-kind contributions (i.e. working on somebody's campaign) could constitute a prohibited contribution; (b) policies/procedures should prohibit use of firm resources (including work hours) to work on a political campaign; (c) testing procedures should be heightened for those known to be involved in the political process; and (d) the SEC considers a state Treasurer and the Governor to be in positions to award business under the pay-to-play rules. We expect the SEC to test firm's policies/procedures under Rule 206(4)-5 during upcoming exams.

Private Equity Firm Violated Pay-to-Play and Registration Rules (*In re TL Ventures*; 6/23/14)

A private equity firm was censured, fined, and order to disgorge fees for violating the pay-to-play rule and erroneously claiming a registration exemption. The SEC alleges that an employee of the respondent made campaign contributions to candidates for mayor and governor, each of which appointed members to the bodies that invested public pension funds. The pay-to-play rule prohibits a firm from receiving compensation during the 2-year period following the contributions. The SEC also charges the firm for claiming an adviser registration exemption where its assets should have been aggregated with an affiliate that was under common control and shared management and operations.

Private equity firms need to take seriously their Advisers Act's compliance responsibilities. More significant than the disgorgement, this firm will now have to explain to its institutional clients and prospects why it has a public enforcement order against it. Also, the SEC will heavily scrutinize an unregistered fund sponsor that "takes a position" that it does not need to register.

E. <u>Cherry-Picking</u>. Don't allocate trades to benefit yourself to the detriment of clients.

Investment Adviser Sentenced to 2 Years in Prison for Cherry-Picking Trades (*SEC v. Strategic Capital Management*; 6/26/17)

An investment adviser was sentenced to 2 years in prison plus another 2 years of supervised release for engaging in an illegal cherry-picking scheme that favored his personal accounts over his clients. He was also ordered to pay $1.3 Million in restitution. The SEC charged that the adviser used omnibus accounts and allocated trades at the end of the trading day. The SEC has not yet imposed civil penalties, which will likely include a significant financial penalty and an industry bar.

When we reported this case back in January, we noted that the SEC included 10b-5 charges to allow for criminal prosecution. Apparently, this strategy was successful as the defendant faces 2 years behind bars.

State-Registered Adviser Barred and Fined for Cherry-Picking (*In re Valor Capital Management*; 3/12/18)

The SEC fined and barred the principal of a state registered adviser for cherry-picking trades to favor his personal accounts over client accounts. The adviser used an omnibus account at two different brokerage firms over a 3-year period to engage in day trading. The SEC asserts that the adviser allocated trades after the relevant security's intraday price changed. The SEC maintains that the trading outcomes indicate a statistically significant allocation to personal accounts. Over the period, the respondent's first day allocations resulted in 81.9% profitable trades to his personal account but only 16% to client accounts. The brokerage firms closed his omnibus accounts because they suspected cherry-picking, although they did not inform the respondent why they terminated. A third brokerage firm did not allow omnibus accounts.

State-registered advisers are not subject to SEC exam or the compliance rule (206(4)-7), which requires a compliance program that includes annual testing and reporting. As a consequence, an adviser that is not SEC registered can go several years engaging in clearly illegal conduct without detection.

F. <u>Proprietary Products</u>. Advisers have a high burden when moving clients into proprietary products.

Large Bank to Pay $267 Million for Investing in Proprietary Funds. (*In re JP Morgan*; 12/22/15)

A large bank admitted wrongdoing and agreed to pay $267 Million in disgorgement, interest and penalties for failing to fully disclose its preference for proprietary funds in managed account programs. The SEC charges the respondents with failing to disclose that the programs were designed and operated with the intent of preferring the firm's own funds, which financially benefitted the firm, even though the firm did disclose that it benefitted from investing in proprietary funds. The respondent's affiliates invested 1/3 to 1/2 of client assets in proprietary funds over a 6-year period. The firm failed to include full disclosure even though the disclosure issue "was raised and discussed" among firm personnel. The SEC also faults the firm for choosing more expensive fund share classes than others available and for failing to disclose revenue sharing received from certain private funds.

When a fiduciary engages in conflicts of interest by investing client assets in proprietary products, the SEC will closely scrutinize the timing, content, and presentation of relevant disclosure. Although the SEC does not specifically prohibit recommending proprietary products, no amount of disclosure may be enough to satisfy the SEC staff.

Adviser Pays $8.9 Million for Allowing Bankers to Influence Manager Selection (*In re Merrill Lynch*; 8/21/18)

A large investment adviser affiliated with a global bank agreed to pay $8.9 Million in disgorgement, fines and interest for allowing affiliated investment banking relationships to influence the selection of a portfolio manager recommended to retail clients. The adviser's due diligence team had recommended the termination of a third party money manager because of personnel changes. According to the SEC, senior executives, seeking an investment banking mandate with the third party, lobbied and influenced the due diligence group to delay the termination until after the awarding of the mandate. The SEC faults the respondent for allowing this conflict of interest to influence its fiduciary obligations to recommend investment products in the best interest of its retail clients.

Compli-pros face enormous challenges in large, global institutions to ferret out multi-lateral business relationships and ensure that the firm adequately observes its fiduciary obligations.

SEC Sues RIA for Moving Clients into Proprietary Mutual Funds (*SEC v. Momentum*; 6/3/16)

The SEC commenced civil enforcement proceedings against an RIA and its principal for moving client assets to proprietary mutual funds[19]. The SEC asserts that the respondent created mutual funds to collect additional fees rather than continue to use third-party ETF models. The SEC avers that the clients paid an additional 115-145 basis points "for no additional services." The respondent's Form ADV did indicate that clients would pay higher fees if they invested in the proprietary mutual funds, but the SEC faults the firm for not disclosing the conflict of interest when the respondent moved assets into higher-expense, but equivalent, strategies that benefitted the adviser but resulted in no additional services to the clients.

Sometimes disclosure cannot cure conflicts of interest. It appears that the SEC has more issue with the higher expense proprietary funds

---

19   The firm and its principals agreed to pay penalties and disgorgement.

> *without additional services rather than the disclosure deficiency. The SEC implies a fiduciary standard that requires advisers to use the lowest-cost product unless it can justify the higher expenses.*

G. <u>Mismanaging Client Assets</u>. Don't ignore mandates, steal assets, churn accounts, or double charge for the same service.

SEC Warns Advisers about Fee and Expense Practices (4/13/18)

The SEC's Office of Compliance Inspections and Examinations has issued a Risk Alert detailing investment adviser failures to properly calculate and disclose fees and expenses. OCIE cites failures to properly value assets, thereby leading to overbilling, using the incorrect fee rate, and billing based on the wrong time period. OCIE also details faulty disclosure practices including Form ADVs that do not reflect actual billing practices and failures to fully disclose compensation arrangements. OCIE also highlights fund sponsors that misallocate expenses. The OCIE findings result from issues identified in deficiency letters issued in recent SEC exams. The Risk Alert advises that firms take action by reimbursing clients and enhancing policies and procedures.

These Risk Alerts often precede enforcement actions. Compli-pros should review their fee billing and disclosure practices in anticipation of an OCIE sweep.

Mutual Fund Manager Fined and Barred from Industry for Investment, Disclosure, and Fee Violations (*In re Balter*; 5/30/17)

A fund manager was barred from the industry and ordered to pay $550,000 for multiple breaches of fiduciary duty including failure to observe the fund's investment limitations. According to the SEC, the respondent did not comply with the fund's investment concentration policies, including the fund's status as "diversified," as described in the Registration Statement and as disclosed to the fund's Board of Directors. The SEC also accuses the respondent, the sole proprietor of the fund manager, with double-charging separate account clients invested in the fund. Additionally, the SEC charges that the respondent cherry-picked trades for his personal benefit to the detriment of clients. The SEC cites violations of the anti-fraud provisions of the Exchange Act, the Advisers Act, and the Investment Company Act.

Registered funds are highly-regulated investment vehicles that require strict adherence to the Investment Company Act, SEC rules, the Registration Statement, and the Board of Directors. Advisers have much less flexibility with respect to disclosure and fees than separate accounts or private funds.

Adviser's Multiple Roles Allowed Misappropriation of Client Funds (*SEC v. Rogicki*; 10/23/17)

The SEC commenced proceedings against an investment adviser who allegedly used his position as trustee and executor of his client's estate and president and co-trustee of the client's foundation, to misappropriate funds. According to the SEC, the adviser befriended the elderly widow of a longtime client and convinced her to appoint him as her executor and foundation president. After she died, he used his position to move money from her foundation to her estate checking account and then transferred funds to his personal accounts. The SEC asserts that the adviser made more than 200 unauthorized transfers totaling more than $9 Million over a 12-year period. The Manhattan District Attorney has also brought criminal charges.

Whether or not this particular adviser engaged in the alleged illegal activity, one key lesson is that an adviser should never assume multiple conflicting roles as investment adviser, executor of a client's estate, and president of the foundation. The appearance of impropriety alone would be hard to defend if an interested family member second-guesses any transaction.

Adviser Charged with Defrauding Professional Athlete (*SEC v. Drake*; 8/29/17)

The SEC has commenced enforcement proceedings against an adviser that it alleges lied to his professional athlete client about management fees. The SEC asserts that the adviser told representatives of the client that the client paid between .15% and .20% of assets in management fees when the client actually paid 1.00%, resulting in significant payments to the adviser who received 60% of the revenue earned by his firm. According to the SEC, the adviser misled the client and his representatives by using false account statements, forged documents, an impostor acting as a Schwab representative, and multiple misrepresentations in emails and meetings. The client's representatives ultimately contacted Schwab, who then informed his employer. The adviser tried to convince the client to lie on his behalf to protect his job, although the client refused.

This type of case shows the problem with assuming that wealthy people are financially sophisticated. Many wealthy people earn their income in fields (e.g. sports, medicine, technology) that would not necessarily make them qualified to make investment decisions. Instead, these successful professionals rely on advisers who are supposed to act as fiduciaries and protect their clients' interests.

Adviser Looted Trust Accounts and Overcharged Clients (*SEC v. Broidy*, 6/5/17)

The SEC barred an investment adviser from the industry and ordered him to pay over $1.7 Million in disgorgement in part for looting trust accounts for which he served as a trustee. According to the SEC, the adviser sold trust assets and purported to replace those assets with lesser-valued securities in which he had a personal interest. The SEC also accuses the adviser of over-charging management fees and making misrepresentations about conflicts of interest.

This type of misconduct is exactly why the SEC should move forward and require all advisers to obtain third party compliance reviews in an effort to weed out wrongdoers. The custody rule (206(4)-2) deems an adviser to have custody where the adviser serves as the trustee of a trust, and requires an annual surprise examination to verify assets and prevent looting of the trust. Unfortunately, an adviser that is willing to steal from clients probably doesn't prioritize compliance.

H. <u>Robo Guidance</u>. The SEC's Division of Investment Management issued regulatory guidance for the operation of robo-advisers.

SEC Issues Robo Guidance on Disclosures, Suitability, and Compliance (2/24/17)

The SEC's Division of Investment Management has issued regulatory guidance for robo-advisers to meet their disclosure, suitability, and compliance obligations. The IM staff recommends robust disclosures about the algorithm (functions, limitations, risks), overrides, third parties, fees, and client information. The staff also urges robo-advisers to adequately disclose limits on the models and to ensure that all disclosures are sufficiently clear and prominent. The staff stresses that robo-advisers must satisfy their suitability obligations by ensuring adequate and clear questionnaires, which would include a process to reconcile inconsistent responses. The Guidance requires robo-advisers to enhance their compliance programs to include policies and procedures to test the algorithm, analyze the questionnaires, oversee third parties, ensure proper disclosures, monitor social media, and protect against cyber-threats. The IM Staff warns that it "will monitor these innovations and implement safeguards, as necessary, to help facilitate such developments and protect investors."

The SEC has been taking a hard look at robo-advisers and whether the digital advice model is consistent with securities laws. This Guidance will force many fintechs to increase compliance and operations spending to satisfy all the requirements described in this Guidance Notice.

FIVE ACTION ITEMS:

1. Do not take any compensation other than the fee the client expressly agrees to pay.

2. Use extreme compliance caution when recommending proprietary products.

3. Adopt and implement specific procedures for managing retirement accounts, including IRA switching and fund recommendations.

4. Reconsider the wrap business. At the very least, conduct a deep compliance review with the enforcement cases as guidance.

5. Audit your mutual fund share recommendations to make sure that you recommend the best product available for the client.

TREND

6

Private equity firms are forced to transform their business practices.

The Dodd-Frank Act, ostensibly a response to the financial crisis, required private equity firms to register as investment advisers even though the private equity industry had little or no involvement with the mortgage or credit industries that caused the Great Recession. Having fended off the SEC before, the private equity industry believed that it would once again avoid regulation. Not only did PE firms not contribute to the crisis, but they sold funds only to sophisticated and/or institutional investors. Surely the Advisers Act, designed for retail advisers that provide services to mom and pop, couldn't apply to the elite cliques that provided access to private companies, oil and gas partnerships, and real estate.

The SEC convinced Congress to lump private equity firms in with hedge fund managers and make them subject to supervision. The SEC successfully argued that many retail investors had exposure to PE through corporate and public pension funds, thereby making PE firms responsible for retirement investors. PE firms should act like fiduciaries, the SEC argued, and implement compliance programs, regardless of how they had traditionally conducted business and whether or not their institutional clients accepted those practices. Nearly 1,400 private fund managers registered with the SEC after 2012.

Immediately after passage of Dodd-Frank, the PE industry fell into the five stages of compliance grief. First there was the denial phase: "Surely, Congress will rescind this, or the SEC will give us an exemption." Second, there was anger: "To heck with the SEC. Let them come after us. I will call my congressman and big-time lawyer and swat them away." The bargaining phase came next: "Maybe we are exempt as a venture capital firm or a multi-family office." "Do we have to count committed capital?" Then, PE firms became depressed: "How much is this going to cost?" "How many people do we have to hire?" "The SEC has a twenty-page document request list?" Most firms finally accepted the reality: "Public plan clients are demanding to see our compliance manual and compliance review. They also want to speak with our CCO." "The SEC just called. They will be here on Monday."

At first, the SEC was patient with the PE industry as firms went through these five stages. SEC staff warned them about their new regulatory obligations and gave them time to change their old ways. The SEC put out notices explaining that taking fees without limited partner consent, even if disclosed in the private placement memorandum, would be a prohibited conflict of interest. The staff warned that marketing materials that singled out certain winning investments violated the Advisers Act. They advised against cross-transactions, insider dealings, charging overhead expenses, and stretching the investment mandate. They told them to hire a legitimate Chief Compliance Officer and implement a comprehensive compliance program.

When many firms ignored the SEC's admonitions, the Enforcement Division, driven by a specialized unit, sprang into action. The SEC brought several seven-figure cases against some of the biggest names in the private equity industry, alleging that certain longstanding practices violated the Advisers Act.

> " The SEC brought several seven-figure cases against some of the biggest names in the private equity industry, alleging that certain longstanding practices violated the Advisers Act. "

In many cases, the SEC alleged wrongdoing and ordered restitution and disgorgement based on conduct that occurred long before the Dodd-Frank Act. The SEC has argued that, before 2012, private equity firms operated as investment advisers with a fiduciary duty, even though the law did not require registration. Therefore, preregistration activities still required PE firms to act in the best interest of clients and with full disclosure. In some cases, the long arm of SEC Enforcement has reached back as far as the early 2000s.

PE firms have also struggled to defend practices that may have been adequately disclosed in their private placement memorandums. However, the Advisers Act's fiduciary standard is higher than the 10b-5 materiality disclosure standard. As an example, a firm cannot engage in cross transactions or give insiders preferential access even if the PPM discloses that the PE firm will engage in such practices. Said another way, not all conflicts of interest can be disclosed away.

An early SEC target was the practice of misallocating broken deal expenses, which include sometimes substantial out-of-pocket research expenses, travel costs, professional fees, and other expenses related to failed portfolio transactions. In *Kohlberg Kravis Roberts*, the private equity behemoth agreed to pay $28 Million for allocating broken deal expenses solely to client funds as opposed to co-investing funds established for the benefit of insiders. The SEC charged that KKR did not disclose this allocation to limited partners and did not implement a reasonable compliance program that addressed broken deal expenses. In *Platinum Equity*, the SEC questioned broken deal expense allocations going back as far as 2004, eight years before passage of the Dodd-Frank Act.

The SEC also has issues with portfolio company monitoring fees. The SEC assessed $39 Million in penalties against Blackstone for failing to seek specific approval of certain IPO fees before they were received, even though the firm did disclose that it would receive such fees in its PPM and Limited Partnership Agreement. In *Apollo*, the PE giant agreed to pay $52.7 Million for similar practices (in addition to other alleged self-dealing transactions).

The SEC has also cracked down on the practice of charging funds for overhead expenses. The SEC imposed a regulatory death penalty in its suit against *Alpha Titans* because the firm charged salaries, rent, parking, utilities, computer, and IT expenses to the funds it managed without disclosure in the PPM or the LPA. Settling an issue we are often asked about, the SEC publicly announced its position (as emerged from the suit against Cherokee Investment Partners) that a private equity firm could not charge its compliance expenses to the funds.

Private equity firms should reconsider longstanding PE practices that the SEC would consider conflicts of interest because the firm or its principals benefit from their unique access without offering the same benefits to their clients. For example, the regulator wants to rid the industry of fund-to-fund cross trading that juices valuations for the benefit of insiders or certain favored clients (see, e.g., *In re Paramount Group*). The SEC also wants to end insider loan transactions (see *In re Guggenheim Partners*) and related party transactions (see *In re Fenway Partners*).

Private equity firms must also rethink their valuation and Code of Ethics practices—both SEC priorities that have plagued traditional investment advisers for decades. For example, the SEC has brought several cases in the real estate and oil and gas industries because these hard-to-value assets allowed for too-high book values that have inflated fees and performance (see, e.g., *In re Houston American Energy*). When considering the Code of Ethics, PE firms must seal any leaks that could result in alleged insider trading. In *SEC v. Ellerin & Blumstein*, the SEC charged consultants with misusing material non-public information. Other areas of focus include failures to properly register or to file required forms.

The Dodd-Frank Act is now six years old. By now, every PE firm should have accepted the realities of the fiduciary obligation, full disclosures, compliance programs, and the inevitability of SEC exams.

A. <u>Broken Deal Expenses</u>. The SEC faults private equity managers for failing to disclose broken deal expense allocations.

Private Equity Firm Will Pay $28 Million to Settle Expense Allocation Charges (*In re Kohlberg Kravis Roberts*; 6/30/15)

A large private equity firm agreed to pay over $28 Million in disgorgement, penalties and interest for failing to allocate broken deal expenses to co-investing funds created for "its executives, certain consultants and others." According to the SEC, from 2006-2011, the respondent did not allocate to these funds broken deal expenses including research costs, travel costs, professional fees, and other expenses relating to deal sourcing. Although the Limited Partnership Agreement permitted the allocation of broken deal expenses to the client fund, the SEC faults the firm because neither the LPA nor any other disclosure document informed clients that the respondent would not allocate broken deal expenses to the co-investing funds. The SEC also charges that the firm failed to implement an adequate compliance program because it did not have reasonable policies and procedures related to the allocation of broken deal expenses. Although the firm did not register until 2008, the SEC disgorgement includes fee allocations that occurred back to 2006.

This case should receive significant attention because of the size of the monetary sanctions, the scrutiny of internal expenses, the failure to implement an adequate compliance program, and the review of activities that occurred before the firm registered. Private equity firms must take action now to prepare for SEC scrutiny of all current and past operations and practices.

PE Firm Pays $3.4 Million for Broken Deal Expenses Paid Since 2004 (*In re Platinum Equity Advisors*; 9/22/17)

A private equity firm agreed to pay over $3.4 Million to settle charges that it failed to allocate broken deal expenses to co-investment funds as far back as 2004. The private equity funds reimbursed the respondent for broken deal expenses including costs incurred to develop, negotiate, and structure potential transactions that were never consummated. The SEC faults the firm, which registered in 2012, for failing to disclose that the funds would pay the broken deal expenses allocable to co-investment vehicles utilized by insiders. The SEC asserts violations of the Advisers Act's antifraud provision (206(2)) and the compliance rule (206(4)-7) for failing to implement a written compliance policy or procedure governing broken deal expense allocation practices.

The SEC reaches all the way back to 2004 to calculate disgorgement even though the firm did not register until 2012. Private fund firms that registered in 2012 should re-examine their expense allocation practices for years prior to 2012 and consider LP reimbursement before the SEC brings a public enforcement case.

B. **<u>Portfolio Monitoring Fees.</u> The SEC has maintained that private equity firms must disclose and obtain LP consent before taking accelerated portfolio monitoring fees.**

Private Equity Firm to Pay $39 Million for Inadequate Fee Disclosures (*In re Blackstone*; 10/8/15)

A large private equity firm agreed to pay nearly $39 Million in disgorgement and fines for failing to disclose accelerated portfolio monitoring fees and taking advantage of legal fee discounts. The SEC alleges that the respondent accelerated portfolio monitoring fees following the sale or IPO of a portfolio company without the required disclosure and consent. Although the firm disclosed that it would receive portfolio monitoring fees in the PPMs and LPAs and disclosed the accelerated fees after receipt (which was subject to rejection by the Limited Partners committee), the SEC asserts that the firm engaged in an unlawful conflict of interest by failing to fully disclose (and obtain consent to) the accelerated fees before receipt. The SEC also asserts that the firm benefitted from legal fee discounts that did not similarly benefit fund investors. The SEC charges that the firm breached its fiduciary duty and failed to implement necessary compliance policies and procedures.

This is the type of technical enforcement action that the industry fears. The respondent disclosed the monitoring fees both before and after receipt. The crux of the SEC's charge is that the firm didn't specifically disclose the acceleration of the monitoring fees upon a sale/IPO event. Rather than simply accept the firm's self-correction for future funds,

the SEC imposed $39 Million in disgorgement and fines. We recommend that every SEC registrant undergo a mock audit and implement a state-of-the-art compliance program including a Chief Compliance Officer with direct Advisers Act experience. It will cost a lot less than $39 Million.

SEC Wallops Large Private Equity Firm with $52.7 Million in Penalties (*In re Apollo*; 8/24/16)

A large private equity firm agreed to pay $52.7 Million in fines, disgorgement, and interest for failing to properly disclose the acceleration of portfolio monitoring fees and certain affiliated loan interest accruals and failing to prevent the reimbursement of unauthorized personal expenses. Although the respondent disclosed that it would receive portfolio monitoring fees, the SEC faults the firm for failing to disclose its practice of accelerating such fees upon sale or IPO until after the commitment of capital and receipt of fees. The SEC also maintains the firm failed to properly disclose interest allocations for certain intercompany loans. The SEC also asserts that the firm's weak compliance program allowed a senior partner to harm the funds by obtaining reimbursement for unauthorized personal expenses, which ultimately led to his separation from the firm. The SEC's Enforcement Director, Andrew J. Ceresney, chided the private equity industry: "A common theme in our recent enforcement actions against private equity firms is their failure to properly disclose fees and conflicts of interest to fund investors."

The SEC continues its enforcement campaign against the private equity industry, notching another 8-figure case. The only real defense is to hire or retain professional compli-pros, conduct a thorough compliance review, and implement a state-of-the-art compliance infrastructure that compares favorably with the traditional asset management industry, which has been subject to the compliance rule since 2005.

Large Private Equity Firm to Pay $12.8 Million for Accelerated Portfolio Monitoring Fees (*In re TPG Capital*; 12/26/17).

A large private equity firm agreed to pay over $12.8 Million in disgorgement, interest and fines for taking accelerated monitoring fees arising from the sale, IPO, and exit from portfolio companies. The PE firm disclosed in the PPM that it would receive portfolio monitoring fees and disclosed in LP reports and the ADV that it received accelerated fees. Nevertheless, the SEC faults the respondent for failing to disclose the accelerated fees before LPs committed capital and failed to submit the accelerated fees to the LP committee for approval. The SEC accuses the firm of engaging in undisclosed conflicts of interest and failing to implement an adequate compliance program.

The SEC has attacked PE fees and expenses including portfolio monitoring fees, broken deal expenses, overhead costs, and consulting fees. To avoid these issues, PE firms may want to re-think their business models and include all fees and expenses in a higher management fee and carried interest.

PE Firm Pays $6.5 Million to Settle Conflict Allegations over Portfolio Consulting Fees (*In re THL Managers*; 7/9/18)

A private equity firm agreed to pay over $6.5 Million in disgorgement, interest and fines for failing to adequately disclose, before commitment of capital, that it would receive accelerated portfolio consulting fees upon IPO or sale of the applicable portfolio company. The PE firm did disclose in the Limited Partnership Agreement that it received portfolio consulting services and disclosed in its Form ADV that it received accelerated fees. Fees were also described in the funds' annual reports and in a side letter for one of the funds. Also, the PE firm credited a large percentage of the accelerated fees against future management fees. However, the SEC faults the firm for neglecting to inform all limited partners before committing capital that it would accelerate portfolio consulting/advisory fees upon IPO or sale for based on the present value of contract fees that could extend up to 10 years. The SEC asserts that only the limited partnership committee could approve these potentially conflicted transactions.

The SEC has brought several cases charging PE firms with taking various forms of ancillary fees (e.g. portfolio monitoring, broken deal expenses, overhead expenses). PE firms should reconsider these ancillary fees in favor of a more inclusive management fee.

C. <u>Overhead Expenses</u>. The SEC will not abide PE firms that charge overhead expenses to the funds.

Death Penalty for Fund Manager that Charged Overhead Expenses to Funds (*In re Alpha Titans*; 4/30/15)

The SEC imposed the death penalty on a fund-of-funds and barred and fined its principals, including its General Counsel, for paying operational expenses out of the funds the firm managed. According to the SEC, certain feeder funds managed by the adviser paid the adviser's operational expenses including salaries and benefits, rent, parking, utilities, computer equipment, and IT services. The SEC asserts that the limited partnership agreements did not authorize the payment of such operational expenses and that general PPM disclosure did not constitute sufficient authorization. Also, the firm's Form ADV did not disclose the payments as additional adviser compensation. The SEC charged the CEO, who also served as the Chief Compliance Officer, and the General Counsel, whom the SEC noted came from a small law firm focused on employment law. To settle the charges, the respondents agreed to fines, industry bars, and a winding up of the firm's operations under the supervision of an independent monitor. The SEC also charged and barred the audit partner of the firm that prepared the funds' financial statements.

OUR TAKE

The SEC has previously stated that it will crack down on private fund managers charging overhead to funds. Although the SEC asserts lack of sufficient disclosure, we believe that no amount of disclosure will be enough to allow the charging of overhead expenses to clients. The implicit message is that you can only charge clients your management fees.

Private Equity Firm Charged Overhead and Portfolio Expenses to Fund (*In re Potomac Asset Management Company*; 9/12/17)

The SEC fined and censured a private equity manager and its principals for unlawfully charging the fund both portfolio company expenses and adviser overhead expenses. The PE manager charged the fund certain consulting expenses provided to a portfolio company without offsetting the management fee as required by the LPA. The PE manager also charged overhead expenses including employee compensation, rent, and the costs of responding to the SEC examination/enforcement. The SEC charges that the expenses were not authorized in the fund's organizational or disclosure documents. The SEC asserts violations of the Advisers Acts antifraud provisions as well as the compliance rule (206(4)-7) for failing to adopt and implement reasonable policies and procedures. As part of its remediation, the PE firm agreed to hire a new Chief Compliance Officer.

It really is better to build a legitimate compliance infrastructure before the SEC arrives rather than in response to an enforcement action. An ounce of compliance prevention can avoid the reputation-crushing havoc of an SEC enforcement action.

PE Firm Failed to Properly Disclose Compliance Expenses Charged to Funds (*In re Cherokee Investment Partners*; 11/9/15)

Two related private equity firms were censured and fined for allocating compliance and legal expenses to the funds they managed without sufficient disclosure. According to the SEC, the respondents charged to the funds over $450,000 in compliance consulting and legal expenses incurred for SEC registration and responding to an SEC exam and investigation. The SEC faults the respondents because the limited partnership agreements did not specifically disclose that the funds "would be charged for a portion of the advisers' own legal and compliance expenses," even though the LPAs did state that the funds would be charged expenses that "arose out of the operation and activities" of the funds.

Consistent with this action, we have generally advised that firms refrain from charging firm compliance and legal expenses to the fund. However, the SEC leaves the door open by stating that the fault lies not in charging the compliance expenses but failing to include specific disclosure in the LPAs.

PE Firm Pays Over $1.6 Million for Improper Expense Allocation (*In re Capital Dynamics*; 8/18/17)

A private equity fund has agreed to pay over $1.6 Million in fines and client reimbursement for misallocating expenses to its fund. The SEC charges that the PE firm unlawfully charged legal, hiring, and employee and consulting expenses to the fund. The SEC interprets the organizational documents as only permitting "normal operating expenses," including "all routine, recurring expenses incident to" their own operations. The SEC faults the firm for failing to adopt and implement appropriate compliance procedures including multiple levels of expense review, escalation procedures and oversight.

PE firms continue to struggle with expense allocation issues, failing to understand that a fiduciary cannot use a managed fund as a piggy bank to pay firm expenses. Proper compliance procedures should prevent firms from crossing the fiduciary line.

PE Senior Partner Expensed Personal Items to Funds (*SEC v. Rashid*; 10/26/17)

The SEC commenced enforcement proceedings against the former senior partner of a large private equity firm for charging personal expenses to the funds he advised. According to the SEC, the senior partner used his corporate credit card for personal expenses that his firm allocated to the funds. The funds' governing documents allowed reimbursement for expenses incurred relating to investments and operations including out-of-pocket expenses for business and travel expenses. Although the conduct occurred over a 3-year period and the company detected unlawful expenses, the senior partner continued to submit false expense reports for which he was reimbursed. The firm ultimately terminated the senior partner after he reimbursed the funds for over $290,000 in personal expenses.

Private equity firms could avoid these problems by only charging management fees (and carry) and end this practice of charging the fund for out-of-pocket expenses. Any expense reimbursement issues would be the private matter between the firm and its employees.

PE Firm Fined $3.5 Million and Reimburses Clients over $8 Million (*In re First Reserve Management*; 9/16/16)

The SEC fined a private equity firm $3.5 Million for engaging in several prohibited conflicts of interest. The respondent also voluntarily agreed to reimburse investors over $8 Million. The SEC alleges that the firm, without disclosure or approval of the LP advisory board, created a structure whereby fund investors paid organizational and operating expenses incurred in the creation of advisory affiliates. The SEC also accuses the fund manager with allocating a disproportionate share of insurance policy premiums to the funds and for benefitting from legal fee discounts. The SEC asserts that the firm's failed compliance program allowed the conflicts to continue. The firm reimbursed investors following discovery of the conflicts during an SEC exam.

 Reimbursing investors after the SEC staff accuses your firm of wrongdoing won't avoid an enforcement action or fines. Private equity firms must implement a robust compliance program that proactively uncovers, reports, and remedies conflicts of interest

D. **Cross Transactions and Conflicts. The SEC has brought several cases alleging undisclosed/unapproved cross transactions and other conflicts of interest.**

1. *Cross transactions*

Unregistered Fund Manager Looted Fund by Inflating Value of Underlying Security (*SEC v. Lester*; 8/8/17)

The SEC fined and barred from the industry the principal of a purported private equity firm for looting one fund to pay another by inflating the valuation of an underlying security transferred between the funds. The SEC pleads that the defendant transferred a worthless interest in a start-up company to one of the funds and then had another fund buy that interest at a $2.8 Million valuation in order to pay off investors in the transferring fund. The SEC contends that the defendant failed to (i) properly value the security with third-party input, (ii) disclose the inherent conflicts of interest and (iii) comply with statements made in the offering memorandum. Neither the fund manager nor the principal were registered in any capacity, but the SEC was able to uncover the wrongdoing as a result of litigation brought by the Colorado Division of Securities.

The state securities regulators serve a valuable function ferreting out fraud and other wrongdoing by firms that fail to register with the SEC and might otherwise go undetected.

Cross-Transaction Was Not Consistent with Disclosure to LP Committee (*In re Paramount Group*; 7/12/17)

The SEC fined and censured a registered real estate private equity firm for engaging in a cross transaction between two funds it managed on terms that differed from those disclosed to its LP committee. According to the SEC, the fund manager committed to the selling fund's investor advisory committee (IAC) that the purchasing fund would reimburse the selling fund for certain development expenses related to the subject property. The fund manager later determined that the selling price already assumed the development costs and, therefore, declined to reimburse the selling fund. However, the fund manager never disclosed to the IAC that it would not reimburse the selling fund. When the transaction was uncovered during an SEC exam, the fund manager paid $4.5 Million to reimburse the selling fund's limited partners.

Private equity firms can overcome conflicts of interest through disclosure to, and consent by, an independent LP committee. However, hiding the ball from the LP committee can result in significant penalties and make your firm look less than transparent.

Hedge Fund Manager Used New Funds to Pay Expenses of Old Funds (*SEC v. Southridge Capital*; 8/17/17)

A hedge fund manager agreed to pay $7.9 Million in disgorgement and a $5 Million fine for using the assets of newer funds to pay the expenses of older funds. According to the SEC complaint, which was filed in 2010 and related to allocations made between 2005 and 2008, the respondent used assets from more recent funds to pay legal and administrative fees of older funds that could not raise cash because they held illiquid securities. The SEC claims that the respondent replaced the cash with overvalued illiquid securities. The SEC continues litigation with respect to charges that the hedge fund manager overvalued securities and made misrepresentations.

The long arm of the law can reach back a long way. The older funds began to have liquidity problems as far back as 2004, which caused the respondent to raise more assets to pay off old expenses. And, the litigation continues.[20]

Fund Manager Failed to Disclose Investments into Affiliate Fund (*In re Columbia River Advisors*; 7/31/17)

The SEC censured and fined a private fund manager for failing to disclose that one of its funds invested in an affiliate fund formed to help grow the manager's business by acquiring other advisers. Although the respondent ultimately made disclosure through the fund's financial statements, the audited financials were delivered 9 months after they were required to be delivered pursuant to the Advisers Act's custody rule (206(4)-2). Also, the firm failed to retain an auditor subject to PCAOB inspection, as required by the Advisers Act. The SEC noted that advisory clients would not have paid any fees had they invested directly in the acquisition fund rather than through the fund in which they intended to invest, which was focused on foreign currencies.

Failure to disclose cross-transactions between affiliate funds will not go undetected. Eventually, the fund manager must deliver audited financial statements, which will require disclosure. The Advisers Act requires advance disclosure (and consent) of conflicts transactions. There is no win in kicking the disclosure down the road until financials are completed.

2. Insider loans

Private Equity Firm Pays $20 Million Fine for Compliance Shortfalls (*In re Guggenheim Partners*; 8/11/15)

A private equity firm agreed to pay a $20 Million fine for failing to adopt and implement reasonable compliance policies and procedures. The firm

---

20   The respondent ultimately agreed to pay $13 Million in disgorgement and penalties as final settlement.

also agreed to retain an independent compliance consultant and deliver the enforcement order to every client and prospective client. The SEC alleges that the firm's weak compliance program resulted in failures to disclose insider loan transactions, report required gifts, maintain required books and records, and properly document trade errors. The SEC says that the firm relied on its parent company for legal and compliance support and that certain issues were not properly reported to, and addressed by, the compliance staff.

Private equity firms that register as investment advisers should retain dedicated and experienced Advisers Act compli-pros to implement the compliance program. Corporate legal or compliance personnel may not have the focus, resources, or knowledge to satisfy the Adviser's Act myriad requirements. Firms that fail to take compliance seriously risk significant public exposure and financial penalties that can have a long-range effect in a competitive marketplace.

Lack of Compliance Infrastructure Costs Private Equity Firm and Principals (*In re Resilience*; 6/30/17)

The SEC fined a private equity firm and its principals, and barred the former CFO/CCO from the industry, for engaging in multiple conflicts of interest transactions with the funds. According to the SEC, prohibited transactions included (i) borrowing from the funds, (ii) failing to make capital contributions, and (iii) using false bookkeeping adjustments to hide transactions. The transactions violated the LPA and were not properly disclosed in capital call notices or financial statements. In addition to anti-fraud and books and records violations, the SEC charged violations of the compliance rule (206(4)-7) because the compliance manual did not address conflicts of interest including control by the two principals and related party transactions. As part of the settlement, the firm hired a new CCO, a new general counsel, a new CFO, and an independent compliance consultant.

Hiring a competent CCO before the SEC arrived would likely have avoided the enforcement action and the resulting damage to the firm's business and reputation. It appears that the principals had no sensitivity to the regulatory environment in which they were operating.

Private Equity Exec Barred from Industry for Personal Transaction with Portfolio Company (*In re Devlin*; 7/27/18)

A private equity firm's managing partner, who also served as its Chief Compliance Officer, was barred from the industry and fined for failing to disclose his personal interest in a portfolio company. The SEC alleges that the respondent caused the fund to make a loan to the portfolio company on the condition that the company used a portion of the proceeds to redeem his investment. The SEC faults the executive for failing to disclose the transaction or to obtain consent to it from the limited partnership committee. Neither the fund nor the investors lost money because the portfolio company ultimately sold the notes to an unaffiliated third party.

Without proper disclosure and consent, a transaction that benefits the fund sponsor or its principals will violate the Advisers Act's fiduciary duty whether or not the investors suffered any harm. This case also highlights the perils of the CCO dual-hat model whereby a senior executive with a pecuniary interest also serves as the Chief Compliance Officer, thereby avoiding independent scrutiny.

Adviser Tried to Conceal Loans to Parent Company (*In re Vertical Capital*; 8/23/17)

A mortgage loan adviser and its two principals agreed to pay over $9 Million in disgorgement, interest, and fines for using funds it managed to make loans to the parent of its affiliated advisers and then using straw man transactions in an attempt to conceal the loans. The SEC maintains that the respondent funneled money to the parent company through undocumented, undisclosed, and unlawful loans made by two private funds and a registered closed-end fund. The respondent then tried to repay the loans by laundering mortgage assets through a straw man that bought mortgage loans from one fund and then transferred them to another fund. The misconduct was uncovered when discrepancies arose between the registered fund's collection account and its custody account. The SEC asserts that the respondent misled the Board and investors, thereby violating the antifraud rules as well as the compliance rule.

Making the unauthorized loans was bad enough and would have resulted in breach of fiduciary duty charges. Trying to conceal the loans through straw man transactions led to the fraud charges, which also could have carried criminal penalties if the U.S. Attorney decided to prosecute.

PE Firm Charged with Pre-Registration Misconduct (*In re JH Partners*; 12/7/15)

The SEC censured and fined a private equity firm for allowing principals to make loans to fund portfolio companies without disclosure and consent and other compliance failures. According to the SEC, the firm registered in 2012, but as far back as 2006, firm principals made nearly $62 Million in direct loans to portfolio companies and took senior interests without disclosing the transactions to the LP advisory board. The SEC also faults the firm for allowing funds to invest in the same portfolio company with different seniority rights and for violating concentration restrictions. The SEC credited the firm with resolving the issues following a 2013 SEC examination. The SEC charges the firm with breaching its fiduciary duty and with violating the Advisers Act's general anti-fraud rule (206(4)-8).

Private fund firms should take note that the SEC faulted conduct that occurred 6 years prior to registration, using its broad authority under the anti-fraud rule. Although the SEC credits the firm with quick remediation, the staff still brought a public enforcement action.

3. Related party transactions

PE Firm Will Pay $10 Million for Failing to Disclose Related Party Consulting Contracts (*In re Fenway Partners*; 11/4/15)

A private equity firm and its four principals, including its CFO/CCO, agreed to pay over $10 Million in disgorgement, interest, and fines for failing to disclose related party consulting arrangements. According to the SEC, the respondents executed consulting agreements with portfolio companies for the payment of monitoring fees. The consulting agreements replaced similar agreements whereby the related investment adviser received the monitoring fees but agreed to offset these payments against the advisory fees. The new consulting agreements did not require any offsets. The SEC charges that the firm misled the LP Advisory Board as well as the auditors. The SEC faulted the CFO/CCO for facilitating the transactions, which included signing the consulting agreements.

Registered private equity firms must understand that the fiduciary duty requires putting your clients' interests first, including an obligation of full disclosure of fees. Firms must reject the culture of opacity that predated Dodd-Frank. In this case, it is an interesting hypothetical question whether the LPs would have even objected to the consulting agreements had they known. Also, it is a CCO's job to identify conflicts of interest, not to facilitate them.

Private Equity Firm Owned by Large Institutional Manager Fined $2.3 Million (*In re WL Ross*; 8/25/16)

A private equity firm owned by a large investment manager agreed to pay $2.3 Million to settle charges that it misallocated transaction fee offsets in order to collect more management fees. The respondent also voluntarily agreed to reimburse investors over $11.8 Million. The funds' LPAs and disclosure documents required an offset of management fees by a portion of transaction fees received for services related to portfolio companies. The SEC alleges that, over a 10-year period, the firm failed to disclose that it would allocate a portion of the transaction fees to co-investors, thereby reducing the offset. The firm itself discovered the misallocation during an SEC exam and self-reported. As part of its remediation efforts, the respondent replaced its Chief Compliance Officer, engaged an independent auditor to perform an internal review, and implemented fee review procedures.

The Advisers Act's fiduciary standard is a much higher standard of care than the 10b-5 standard applicable to private equity funds before Dodd-Frank. A practice that might not have been "material" to an investor's initial investment decision could still violate the Advisers Act's more stringent disclosure and fiduciary requirements when the fund sponsor (adviser) benefits financially to the detriment of investors (clients).

PE Firm Censured for Failing to Disclose Investment in Service Provider (*In re Centre Partners*; 1/11/17)

The SEC fined and censured a private equity fund manager for failing to disclose that the principals had personally invested in an IT firm that it had engaged. The respondent utilized the IT firm to perform due diligence before investing in portfolio companies. The SEC asserts that the firm failed to disclose that firm principals invested in the IT firm and occupied Board seats and that the IT firm's CEO is the brother-in-law of one of the principals. Although the SEC acknowledges that neither the PE firm nor the principals profited and that the amount paid to the IT firm was not a material portion of its revenue, the SEC faults the firm for failing to disclose this conflict of interest in the PPMs, ADV, or to the LP Advisory Committee.

The SEC will bring an enforcement action even without any underlying client harm or benefit to the accused. Here, the mere failure to disclose a personal investment results in a public enforcement action.

Private Equity GP Barred and Fined for Charging Undisclosed Fees (*In re SLRA*; 2/8/17)

A private equity manager was barred from the industry and agreed to pay a $1.25 Million fine for taking £16.25 Million in unauthorized fees. The respondents also agreed to reimburse the funds over $24 Million. According to the SEC, the respondent, in its capacity as GP, invoiced the funds for real estate workout fees pursuant to an oral agreement it made with an affiliate. The SEC asserts that the respondents needed additional cash because the financial crisis reduced their fees and increased their workload and expenses, but the LP advisory committee refused. The SEC asserts that the purported agreement with the affiliate was never disclosed to the LPs or the auditors. When the LPs objected to the additional fees, the respondent sued the limited partners but ultimately agreed to reimburse the funds after the SEC's investigation commenced.

Way back when (before Dodd-Frank?), a GP may have had unfettered power to engage in conflicts of interest and assess undisclosed fees. As a fiduciary under the Advisers Act, private equity GPs must seek approval for additional fees and fully disclose all potential conflicts. Otherwise, they won't be a GP for long.

Fund Executive to Pay $2.1 Million for Opaque Trading Practices (*In re James Caird Asset Management*; 6/6/16)

The principal of a private fund manager agreed to pay over $2.1 Million in disgorgement, interest and penalties for failing to fully inform investors about an internal investment opportunity policy that significantly favored a fund in which the principal had a significant economic interest. The SEC maintains that the firm managed a large hedge fund alongside a small opportunistic fund but told investors that the trading strategies would not overlap. However, the firm, controlled by the principal, maintained an internal policy of allocating 1/3 of all new issue opportunities to the small fund and 2/3 to the large fund even though the small fund was 1/20th of the size of the large fund. The SEC asserts that the principal benefited because he owned approximately 20% of the small fund through a family trust. The SEC faults the firm for continuing to create an impression that the trading strategies did not overlap.

Firms that engage in multiple product lines must re-consider their trade opportunity and aggregation policies. Even non-intentional favoritism of one client over another will raise the regulatory eyebrows.

Private Equity GP Received a Percentage of Group Purchasing Arrangement (*In re WCAS Management Company*; 4/26/18)

A private equity sponsor agreed to pay over $770,000 in fines, disgorgement, and interest for failing to obtain prior approval of a group purchasing arrangement that benefited the sponsor. The respondent entered into a group purchasing agreement with a third party organization that negotiated group discounts on business expenses such as rental cars and office supplies. The third party agreed to pay the respondent 25% of net revenue received from the underlying vendors. The SEC asserts that the respondent did not disclose or seek independent limited partner approval for the arrangement, which created an incentive for the sponsor to recommend the services.

Any transaction that benefits the GP that is not specifically disclosed up-front must be approved by all, or a committee of, independent limited partners.

❑ The List: Ten Private Equity Practices that Cause Regulatory Problems

The private equity industry has seen increased SEC scrutiny and several significant enforcement actions since the adviser registration requirement went into effect in 2012. In today's list, we offer ten PE practices that have caused regulatory problems for registered PE firms.

Ten Private Equity Practices that Cause Regulatory Problems

1.	**Direct transactions with portfolio companies.** The SEC will highly scrutinize affiliate loans to portfolio companies, consulting arrangements with affiliates, and insiders serving as officers.
2.	**Varying seniority rights for LPs.** Giving preferential treatment to certain LPs (especially insider coinvestors) will violate a fiduciary's obligation to treat all clients equally.
3.	**Misallocating co-investor expenses.** Insider co-investors must bear the same expense allocations as outside LPs.
4.	**Accelerating portfolio monitoring fees.** The SEC has brought at least two significant cases for failing to fully disclose how LPs will absorb accelerated portfolio monitoring fees incurred after a liquidation event.
5.	**Charging broken deal expenses.** The SEC views this practice as another way for a fiduciary to illegally line its own pockets at the expense of LPs.
6.	**Legal fee discounts.** Getting lower rates from your law firm (and other service providers) because they work on the funds violates your fiduciary duty.
7.	**Overcharging overhead expenses.** Several firms have been cited for taking overhead expenses out of the funds without adequate disclosure.
8.	**Cross-portfolio transactions.** Transactions between funds including interfund lending or cross trading will violate the Advisers Act.
9.	**Not registering as a broker-dealer.** Investment banking activities for portfolio companies require broker-dealer registration.
10.	**Weak compliance program.** Several PE firms failed to hire a competent and dedicated CCO to implement a specific Advisers Act compliance program.

E. <u>Valuation</u>. Firms must fairly value private securities according to reasonable and objective criteria.

Oil and Gas Firm Over-Valued Reserves (*In re Houston American Energy*; 8/5/14)

The SEC has commenced enforcement proceedings against an oil and gas producer and its CEO for over-stating and over-valuing oil reserves.[21] The SEC alleges that the respondents quadrupled the estimates received from the operator and used a price per barrel based on commercially viable wells. Using these inflated numbers, which translated into a higher stock valuation, the respondents raised money from outside investors as the firm's stock price increased. The SEC charges several violations of the anti-fraud rules. The SEC also brought charges against the respondent's marketing consultant for publishing information about a security without fully disclosing the compensation received.

The SEC has increased focus on valuation claims for non-traded assets such as oil and gas reserves and private companies. This scrutiny will likely work its way into exams of private equity firms now registered as investment advisers.

Hedge Fund Manager Over-Relied on Third Party Pricing Service (*In re Covenant Financial*; 3/30/17)

A hedge fund manager agreed to pay disgorgement, investor reimbursement, fines and interest for misvaluing portfolio securities and thereby collecting inflated management fees. According to the SEC, the fund manager relied almost exclusively on a third-party pricing service to value municipal bonds. The pricing service significantly over-priced securities by failing to include observable inputs such as broker quotes. Over the course of at least 2 years, the actual sales prices of bonds were significantly less than their stated valuations. As a result, the fund manager overstated fund NAVs, which caused an overpayment to redeeming shareholders and inflated management fees. The SEC faults the firm for failing to value the municipal bonds in accordance with

---

21   The respondents paid $572,500 in penalties to settle the action.

GAAP (ASC 820) and good faith, as described in its Valuation Policy, financial statements and disclosure documents.

Fair valuation requires a determination of the price that would be received between market participants. A fund manager cannot slavishly rely on a third party pricing service especially if the prices result in an ongoing pattern inconsistent with actual transactions.

F. Failure to Register. Firms are targeted for claiming dubious registration exemptions.

Private Fund Salesperson Pays $22 Million for Failing to Register (*SEC v. Sarafraz*; 5/16/14)

An unlicensed salesperson agreed to pay over $22 Million in disgorgement, penalties, and interest to settle charges that he sold interests in a private fund without registering as a broker-dealer or becoming associated with a broker-dealer. The SEC asserts that the defendant "met with prospective investors in person, spoke with them on the telephone, or communicated via the internet" and that he "described the investment program to investors and recommended they purchase" interests. The SEC claims that the defendant raised over $97 Million and was paid over $18 Million in commissions. The SEC said that it is "committed to holding such unregistered salespeople accountable for their conduct."

As part of its new initiative to examine private fund sponsors, the SEC has indicated that it will look at sales activities to determine whether a firm or a person should register or obtain a securities license. If a person earns their money as a percentage of assets raised and they speak directly with potential investors, registration and/or licensing may be required. Notably, the complaint does not allege that any investors complained or lost money.

Foreign Bank Pays $12.5 Million for Failing to Register as BD/IA (*In re HSBC Private Bank*; 12/1/14)

A large foreign bank agreed to pay $12.5 Million and admit wrongdoing for soliciting and servicing U.S. clients without registering as a broker-dealer or investment adviser. According to the SEC, the bank's relationship managers made several visits to the U.S. in order to service clients over an 8eight-year period. The bank maintained both brokerage and advisory accounts, accepted and executed orders, solicited securities transactions, handled funds, provided account statements, and provided investment advice. The SEC states that the bank failed to implement its own compliance policies even after warnings from its own compliance and internal audit functions and directives from senior management. The SEC indicates that the firm made $5.7 Million in pretax income from the activities.

The SEC has focused on failure to register in recent years. In addition to non-U.S. entities, the SEC has also targeted firms and individuals that conduct private fund solicitation activities. It is also noteworthy that the firm paid more than double the income earned to settle the charges.

SEC Uses Anti-Fraud Rules to Prosecute Unregistered Fund Manager (*SEC v. Varacchi & Sentinel Growth*; 2/6/17)

The SEC has charged an unregistered fund manager with stealing nearly $4 Million in client funds by commingling assets and siphoning off investment funds for personal and business expenses. The SEC asserts that the respondents hid their nefarious activities by providing false account statements that failed to show that the assets were heavily leveraged with margin accounts. Although the respondent was not registered with the SEC or any state, the SEC charges charged violations of Section 10(b) (fraud in connection with purchase/sale of securities); Section 17(a) (fraud in the offering of securities); Sections 206(1) and 206(2) of the Advisers Act (investment adviser fraud); and Rule 206(4)-8 of the Advisers Act (fraud in pooled investment vehicles).

All this talk about repealing Dodd-Frank (see Cipperman podcast) will not stop the SEC from using the anti-fraud rules against fund managers even if they are not registered. The SEC used the anti-fraud rules to pursue private fund manager wrongdoing long before enactment of the Dodd-Frank Act (See, e.g., SEC v. Lawton, (2009)).

Public Company Fined for Operating as Inadvertent Investment Company (*In re Honeysuckle Research*; 10/4/17)

The SEC fined and censured a public company for failing to register as an investment company because over 80 percent of its assets consisted of noncontrolling interests in other OTC companies after the respondent changed business direction in 2014 and began purchasing OTC and private interests in marijuana-related businesses. In 2015, the company could not respond to SEC requests about investment company registration, which is required when investment securities exceed 40 percent of total assets. As a public company, the respondent could not rely on private offering exemptions 3(c)(1) or 3(c)(7). As part of the settlement, the company agreed to register or pay a $5,000 penalty for each month that the company failed to register.

Operating companies engaged in passive investing, which often occurs in emerging industries, must be aware of becoming an inadvertent investment company. Once total investment securities exceed about one quarter of total assets, it's time to consult a 1940 Act lawyer.

RIA's Affiliate Private Fund Manager Wrongly Claimed Registration Exemption (*In re Bradway Financial*; 7/28/17)

The SEC censured and fined a fund manager and its principal and barred the principal from serving as a chief compliance officer for incorrectly claiming exemption from Advisers Act registration and its requirements. The SEC contends that the principal, which managed a registered investment adviser, created an affiliate to manage two private funds and then claimed an exemption from registration because the funds had less than $150 Million. The SEC maintains that the affiliate was required to register because it was under common control with the registered adviser and shared office space, employees and technology. The SEC alleges that the private fund adviser hoped to avoid the custody rule's audit requirements and compliance requirements. The SEC cites Section 208(d) of the Advisers Act, which prohibits a person from doing indirectly any act which would be unlawful if done directly.

This case has significant implications for larger organizations. If a firm operates a registered investment adviser affiliate, the SEC, based on this action's reasoning, would prohibit the firm from claiming an exemption registration for an unregistered fund manager under the same roof. The SEC is using the regulatory flexibility to integrate advisers under one Form ADV as a regulatory weapon to force registration on otherwise exempt affiliates.

Real Estate Interests are "Securities" Triggering Fund Registration (*In re Landwin Management;* 7/17/17)

A purported real estate investment fund violated the Investment Company Act because investments in real estate limited partnership interests and mortgage loans constituted "securities." A fund that invests more than 40% of its assets in securities must register under the Investment Company Act, absent an exemption (e.g. fewer than 100 investors, solely offered to qualified purchasers). According to the SEC, the fund exceeded the 40% threshold when the real estate related securities were added to other publicly-traded stocks and bonds in which the fund invested. The SEC also accused the fund manager and its principal of failing to fully disclose how the fund would invest.

For purposed of the Investment Company Act, the SEC applies a broad interpretation of "security" to include pooled interests in real estate, even though a direct investment in the underlying property would not be counted. Real estate private equity firms should not assume that they can avoid registration without a deeper analysis of their investments.

Adviser Barred for Failing to Register as BD for Private Fund Sales (*In re Smith;* 3/2/17)

A financial adviser was barred from the industry and ordered to pay over $400,000 in disgorgement and interest for failing to register as a broker-dealer while selling interests in a private fund. According to the SEC, the respondent identified investors, communicated with them (including in person), advised prospective investors on the merits of the investment, assisted handling funds, and collected transaction-based commissions. The adviser sold notes issued by a third party fund that ultimately defaulted. The SEC charges that the respondent's activities violated Section 15(a)(1) of the Exchange Act, which requires registration as a broker-dealer to sell securities.

Over the last couple of years, the SEC has increased enforcement efforts to prosecute individuals and firms who sell private funds without registering as, or becoming affiliated with, a broker-dealer.

G. <u>Code of Ethics</u>. PE and hedge firms must think broadly about who should be covered by the code of ethics, personal trading restrictions, and surveillance.

Consultant to PE Portfolio Company Charged with Insider Trading (*SEC v. Ellerin and Blumstein*; 11/16/17)

A consultant to a private equity fund's portfolio company has agreed to pay a fine and disgorgement to settle insider trading charges. According to the SEC, the consultant obtained impending acquisition information from the acquirer's Chief Revenue Officer and traded on the information prior to the acquisition announcement. The SEC also alleges that she passed the information to a friend who also traded. The SEC asserts that the consultant "violated her fiduciary duties or similar obligations arising from a relationship of trust and confidence" to the client company.

Private equity firms registered as investment advisers should ensure that portfolio company officers and consultants comply with the Code of Ethics, including reporting of securities transactions and the obligation to maintain the confidentiality of material nonpublic information.

Hedge Fund Firm Failed to Stop Sharing of Confidential Information (*In re Brahman Capital*; 12/6/17)

The SEC fined and censured a hedge fund firm for failing to stop its research analyst from sharing confidential information with his wife, who ran another hedge fund. The research analyst helped his wife start the competing firm and provided internal confidential information including investment models, research and recommendations. In fact, holdings of the two hedge fund firms significantly overlapped. After the respondent become aware and warned the research analyst about sharing confidential information, it failed to stop the conduct despite policies and procedures about email review and maintaining confidential information. The SEC faults the firm for failing to supervise and for failing to implement an adequate compliance program that would effectively monitor and halt unlawful conduct.

You must walk the compliance walk, not just talk the compliance talk. Registered firms must implement *compliance policies and monitoring, not simply adopt broad policies and procedures that sound good.*

Hedge Fund Misused Inside Information from Affiliate's Research Department (*In re Sidoti & Company*; 2/15/17)

An investment bank was fined and censured for failing to enforce information barriers between its research department and an affiliated hedge fund managed by the bank's CEO. The investment bank maintained policies and procedures related to the misuse of material nonpublic information, including a restricted list applicable to the bank's employees. However, the restricted list did not stop the hedge fund from making 126 trades in restricted list securities over a 6-month period. In response to deficiencies raised during an SEC examination that occurred before the unlawful trading, the hedge fund adopted policies and procedures that applied the restricted list, required physical barriers, instituted email monitoring, and restricted information flow. The SEC alleges that the hedge fund failed to enforce those policies.

Compliance means more than a drafting unused policies and procedures. It means actually enforcing those policies to prevent unlawful conduct. This firm likely incurred the enforcement action because it told the SEC that it had fixed the problem by adopting policies and procedures but then ignored implementation.

H. <u>Filing Forms</u>. Once registered, PE firms must mind the various reporting and filing requirements.

SEC Fines 13 Firms for Failing to File Form PF (*In re Bachrach Asset Management et. al.*; 6/4/18)

The SEC censured and fined 13 private fund managers for failing to file Form PF over multi-year periods. Form PF, required to be filed annually since 2012, requests information about a fund manager's assets under management, fund strategies, performance, leverage, and derivatives. An SEC Enforcement official advised: "We encourage investment advisers to take a fresh look at whether they are meeting their reporting obligations and adjust their compliance programs accordingly."

While some may wonder whether this is a return to "broken windows" enforcement, these cases involved a complete failure to make the Form PF filings over several years, not mere quibbling over definitions and categories. If you don't know what filings you have to make, it's time to hire a compliance officer or a compliance consulting firm.

General Partner Fined for Violating Tender Offer Rules (*In re Genesis Associates*; 7/31/18)

The SEC censured and fined the General Partner of a private partnership for failing to file the required notice and response to third party tender offers. The SEC faults the GP for failing to file a Schedule 14D-9 following the receipt of information of tender offers for more than 5% of the partnership's interests. The Schedule 14D-9 is the method by which investors receive information about a tender offer and management's response. Because no public market existed for the partnership's interests, the failure to notify investors could have resulted in fewer investors selling their interests to the third party.

Closed-end funds that rely on tender offers for investor liquidity must ensure strict compliance with the arcane and voluminous tender offer rules. As the market for more esoteric products grows, the SEC will use the tender offer rules to ensure full and fair disclosure.

Private Equity Firm Failed to Deliver Financials within 120 Days (*In re New Silk Road Advisors*; 7/19/18)

The SEC fined and censured a private equity firm for failing to deliver audited financial statements to limited partners within 120 days of the end of the fiscal year, as required by the custody rule (206(4)-2). The firm missed the deadline by an average of more than 60 days in every year since it registered in 2012. Although the staff will give a firm a pass if it misses the deadline due to "unforeseeable circumstances," the SEC faults the PE firm for failing to make material changes to its compliance processes, thereby leading to a violation in 6 consecutive years.

We have found the staff to be fairly reasonable if a firm misses the deadline by a few days because of an unusual event such as a hard-to-value security or a change in auditors. When you consistently ignore a regulatory requirement and fail to make changes, the Enforcement Division will treat you as a regulatory recidivist and proceed accordingly.

FIVE ACTION ITEMS:

1. Hire a CCO or a compliance firm with experience in asset management; don't rely on deal counsel or in-house M&A counsel for Advisers Act compliance.

2. Consolidate all fees and compensation into the management fee plus carry to avoid any allegations that the firm has received undisclosed payola.

3. Develop allocation procedures that ensure no favorable treatment for particular clients or insiders when considering new investments, expense allocations, and exit transactions.

4. Create an active LP committee that can independently approve transactions.

5. Limit personnel who have access to client and investment information, thereby simplifying Code of Ethics monitoring and reporting.

TREND 7

Cybersecurity and protection of customer information have become top industry priorities.

No issue worries investment firms or regulators more than cybersecurity. With visions of Russian hackers trolling the dark web, regulators want firms to lock down sensitive client information. Investment management execs also worry about proprietary firm information, rogue employees, vendors, and, of course, the regulators. Meanwhile, everybody fears the political and media blowback of a serious breach.

Cybersecurity may be one area where the real risk may exceed the concern. The newspapers describe email hacking, ransomware and phishing attacks, and global viruses. An employee of a large investment bank is accused of stealing customer information and then exposing it to a hacker on his personal computer. A third-party cloud provider is hacked by foreign interests.

The regulators have taken action. OCIE has conducted two industry sweeps to determine cybersecurity readiness. The SEC and FINRA have put out risk alerts and notices about cybersecurity deficiencies and best practices. Both have identified cybersecurity as an examination priority. Disclosure guidelines have been issued for public companies. Enforcement actions have been filed.

Yet confusion persists about the definition of "cybersecurity" and the limits of reasonable cybersecurity precautions. We believe that FINRA has provided the best definition: "protection of investor and firm information from compromise (i.e., loss of data confidentiality, integrity, or availability) through the use—in whole or in part—of electronic digital media." As a touchstone, most IT professionals look to the National Institute of Standards and Technology's "Framework for Improving Critical Infrastructure Cybersecurity."

Over the last couple of years, the SEC and FINRA have crystalized the elements that firms should address in a reasonable cybersecurity readiness plan. These include adequate governance practices (i.e. policies and procedures), periodic risk assessments, reviews of access controls, safeguards against data loss, employee training, vendor supervision, and a detailed incident response plan.

Despite the protests of non-tech-savvy compliance officers, the regulators have made clear that compliance officers own cybersecurity risk like any other regulatory risk. This does not mean that CCOs must understand how to conduct a penetration test. But, it does mean that CCOs must ensure that their firms address the seven elements described above. A CCO cannot offload accountability to the "IT folks" or the cloud provider.

Also, firms cannot escape scrutiny by arguing that they are too small or don't retain client data. The SEC and FINRA want to lock down the

> **The SEC and FINRA want to lock down the entire financial services digital ecosystem to avoid any holes that ill-intentioned hackers could exploit.**

entire financial services digital ecosystem to avoid any holes that ill-intentioned hackers could exploit.

In 2017, the SEC also created its own Cyber Unit within the Enforcement Division. In addition to rooting out cybersecurity vulnerabilities, the Cyber Unit has taken aim at cryptocurrency offerings and has already brought cases against alleged fraudsters for taking advantage of the lack of regulation in the digital token world. The SEC has also placed a moratorium on approving public funds that seek to invest in cryptocurrencies until it resolves several regulatory issues such as disclosure, custody, valuation, and liquidity. One emerging question is whether cryptocurrency offerings are securities subject to SEC jurisdiction.

The SEC and FINRA have held several registrants accountable for their weak cybersecurity practices. In its case against RT Jones Capital, the SEC fined and sanctioned the adviser for violating the Safeguards Rule of Regulation S-P—even though no client suffered harm—because the firm failed to implement necessary procedures to prevent a hack of customer information at its third-party-hosted web server. Morgan Stanley agreed to pay a $1 Million fine because it failed to prevent an employee from misappropriating over 700,000 client accounts. Lincoln Financial paid a $650,000 fine to settle charges that it failed to ensure the security of one of its OSJ's cloud server vendors.

The SEC has also raised concerns about firms that fail to properly disclose data breaches. The Verizon subsidiary formerly known as Yahoo agreed to pay a $35 Million fine for waiting nearly two years before publicly disclosing a data breach that affected over 500 million customers. In the interim, the SEC alleged that Yahoo filed several misleading 10-Qs and 10-Ks. Yahoo also refunded $350 Million to Verizon because of related misrepresentations in the Stock Purchase Agreement.

State-level regulators have also acted to ensure cybersecurity. The large insurance firm Nationwide agreed to pay $5.5 Million to settle charges brought by thirty-two states after criminals hacked into customer data by exploiting a breach created by the company's failure to implement a security patch. The New York attorney general, who received over 1500 data breach notices in 2017, warned that he would "hold companies to account" if they failed to protect customers' personal information.

The Justice Department has also brought criminal penalties. In *Holt*, a financial adviser went to prison because his alleged Ponzi scheme sent emails across state lines, thereby constituting wire fraud.

A. <u>OCIE Cybersecurity Sweep</u>. OCIE conducted its second sweep of cybersecurity readiness and has offered best practices.

SEC Sweep Yields Cybersecurity Best Practices (8/9/17)

The SEC Office of Compliance Inspections and Examinations (OCIE) released the results of its Cybersecurity 2 sweep initiative. OCIE reviewed policies and procedures and assessed cybersecurity preparedness of 75 firms with respect to governance and risk assessment, access rights and controls, data loss prevention, vendor management, training, and incident response. OCIE found that most firms have adopted policies and procedures, conducted penetration tests and vulnerability scans, used a system to prevent data loss, installed software patches, adopted response plans, and conducted vendor risk assessments. OCIE recommended that registrants better tailor policies and procedures, conduct enhanced employee training, replace outdated systems, and ensure remediation of identified vulnerabilities. OCIE warned that cybersecurity "remains one of the top compliance risks for financial firms" and that it "will continue to examine for cybersecurity compliance procedures and controls, including testing the implementation of those procedures and controls at firms."

Advisers, broker-dealers, and funds that fail these compliance best practices risk falling behind their competitors and incurring the wrath of the OCIE examiners. Compliance officers must become conversant in the required elements of an adequate cybersecurity program and implement the required policies and procedures, testing, and remediation.

❑ *The List: The Twelve-Step Cybersecurity Program*

The Twelve-Step Cybersecurity Program:

1.	**Identify the location of confidential information.** Conduct an internal assessment of the location of confidential information and who might have access.
2.	**Restrict access.** Passwords should be specific to each employee and should require updating on a periodic basis. Also, make sure to shut down access for exiting employees.
3.	**Monitor for intrusions.** The IT function should add intrusion monitoring as part of the virus and security protocols. Also, IT should report multiple log-in failures.
4.	**Prohibit removable storage media.** Also, create a hardware environment that makes it difficult to use such media.
5.	**Limit devices.** Only firm-approved and encrypted devices should have access to the network/system.
6.	**Test vulnerability.** Hire an IT firm to perform a vulnerability assessment and conduct penetration testing.
7.	**Evaluate vendors.** Ensure vendor selection includes due diligence of the vendor's cybersecurity infrastructure. Create an ongoing monitoring and reporting system.
8.	**Report to Management.** Add cybersecurity as an agenda item to every management and compliance meeting, and include reports from IT and compliance.
9.	**Appoint somebody accountable.** One person should own cybersecurity compliance across the organization, whether that person resides in IT, compliance, or operations.
10.	**Create response plan.** The response plan should include required notices to clients and regulators and how to patch vulnerabilities.
11.	**Consider cybersecurity insurance.** Determine if a cybersecurity insurance policy will protect the firm against a catastrophic event.
12.	**Implement policies and procedures.** Develop policies and procedures governing all of the above and annually test whether they are being followed. Also, ensure ongoing employee training.

B. <u>SEC Cyber Unit</u>. The SEC has created a dedicated unit within the Enforcement Division to focus on cybersecurity and fraud.

SEC Creates Cyber-Unit (9/26/17)

The SEC's Enforcement Division has created a new Cyber Unit targeting "cyber-related misconduct." The new Cyber-Unit will target market manipulation schemes using electronic and social media, hacking schemes, account intrusions, and the dark web. The Co-Director of the SEC's Enforcement Division labeled cyber-related threats as one of the "greatest risks facing investors and the securities industry."

We suspect that this Cyber Unit will ultimately morph into its own office (See OCIE, Whistleblowers). If you have been on vacation in the woods for the last 3 years and have not yet retained a third-party firm to test your cybersecurity readiness, we recommend moving quickly to catch up to the rest of the industry.

SEC's Cyber Unit Stops Virtual Currency Offering (*SEC v. PlexCorps*; 12/5/17)

The SEC obtained an emergency asset freeze against a fraudulent internet-based initial coin offering. According to the SEC, the Canadian respondents promised outlandish returns and made other significant misrepresentations as part of a scheme that raised over $15 Million from thousands of investors through offerings of a crypto-currency advertised on various social media sites. The SEC asserts that the offering of virtual tokens constituted an illegal offering of securities and that it was made available to U.S. investors through the internet. The SEC announced that this case is the first filed by its new Cyber Unit, which was created in September to focus on "misconduct involving distributed ledger technology and initial coin offerings, the spread of false information through electronic and social media, hacking and threats to trading platforms."

Perhaps most significant is the SEC asserting (without much precedent or support) that an initial coin offering is an offering of securities subject to the securities laws. This view may lead to broader regulatory

oversight of cryptocurrency offerings. Also, we expect that this first action by the Cyber Unit won't be its last.[22]

SEC Raises Cryptocurrency Fund Questions (1/22/18)

The SEC's Division of Investment Management sent a letter to the ICI and SIFMA listing the "significant outstanding questions" concerning how proposed registered funds investing in cryptocurrencies and related products would satisfy the Investment Company Act. The letter, signed by Division Director Dalia Blass, warned potential fund sponsors against initiating fund registrations until these questions "can be addressed satisfactorily." The letter questions how funds would value cryptocurrencies and related products given their volatility and lack of regulation. The Division also questions liquidity and whether funds could meet daily redemption requests. The letter also raises custody concerns, asking how funds could "validate existence, exclusive ownership, and software functionality." ETFs pose additional questions related to authorized participant and arbitrage processes. The letter also asks about distribution and fiduciary duty. The Division expressed its willingness to "engage in dialogue with sponsors regarding the potential development of these funds."

We believe that both the industry and the SEC have vested interests in coming to an agreement to allow cryptocurrency offerings. The industry should welcome prudent regulation, which gives investors the type of confidence that made mutual funds so successful. The SEC should get out in front of this issue to become the regulator of choice rather than cede its regulatory authority to offshore, non-U.S., and private markets.

SEC Warns Advisers and Broker-Dealers to Protect against Ransomware (5/18/17)

The SEC's Office of Compliance Inspections and Examinations (OCIE) issued a Risk Alert about recent ransomware attacks and offered some

---

22   The SEC has brought several other cases against alleged ICO fraudsters.

best practices for smaller firms for dealing with ransomware incidents. Based on a recent review of 75 registrants, the OCIE staff recommends that firms perform a cyber-risk assessment, conduct penetration and vulnerability tests, and ensure software maintenance including adequate software patches. The OCIE staff stressed the importance of developing a "rapid response capability." OCIE found widespread deficiencies among advisers during its review: 57% did not conduct penetration and vulnerability testing and 26% did not conduct periodic risk assessments of critical systems.

Cybersecurity has become one of the most significant compliance issues facing investment management firms. CCOs and their bosses must take action to address outside threats. We recommend reviewing the SEC's 2014 guidance.

SEC Issues Cybersecurity Compliance and Disclosure Guidance (2/23/18)

The SEC has issued cybersecurity guidance that directs public companies to adopt effective disclosure controls and procedures and overhaul their disclosure about incidents and threats. The SEC believes that public companies should adopt and implement cybersecurity risk management policies and procedures that ensure timely disclosure, internal reporting, processing of risks and incidents, and prevention of insider trading. The SEC also admonishes public companies to review all public disclosures including the materiality of incidents and security, risk factors, MD&A disclosure, business description, legal proceedings, financial statements, and board risk oversight. Firms should also consider disclosing past incidents "in order to place discussions of these risks in the appropriate context." The SEC believes that "the importance of data management and technology to business is analogous to the importance of electricity and other forms of power in the past century." The SEC said that it will be reviewing cybersecurity disclosures.

We expect institutional investors will add similar cybersecurity inquiries into their Operational Due Diligence processes before choosing an investment firm. So, even if you do not work for a public company, you should consider implementing the SEC's recommendations.

C. <u>Enforcement Actions for Weak Cyber Controls</u>. The SEC and FINRA have brought cases against advisers who have failed to implement adequate cybersecurity controls.

SEC Punishes RIA for Failing to Stop Cyber Attack (*In re R. T. Jones Capital*; 9/24/15)

The SEC fined and sanctioned an investment adviser for failing to adopt policies and procedures reasonably designed to protect confidential client information from a hacker. The SEC asserts that a foreign cyber-intruder gained access to customers' names and social security information housed at its third party-hosted web server. Although no clients suffered financial harm, the SEC charges the firm with violating the Safeguards Rule (Rule 30(a) of Regulation S-P) by failing to conduct periodic risk assessments, employing a firewall, encrypting client data, and establishing procedures to respond to a cybersecurity incident. The Co-Chief of the SEC Enforcement Division's Asset Management Unit, Marshall S. Sprung, said "As we see an increasing barrage of cyber attacks on financial firms, it is important to enforce the safeguards rule even in cases like this when there is no apparent financial harm to clients."

Although it may be difficult/impossible to stop cyber attacks especially at a third party, firms must adopt policies and procedures to create a legal defense that it did all that was reasonable despite an attack. We expect that many firms will struggle with the costs and implementation of enhanced cyber-security.

Large BD/RIA Fined $1 Million for Cybersecurity Breach (*In re Morgan Stanley*; 6/9/16)

A large broker-dealer/investment adviser agreed to pay a $1 Million fine because its technology safeguards failed to prevent an employee from downloading and misappropriating personal customer information. The SEC asserts that the employee found a weakness in the firm's authorization procedures, thereby allowing him to access customer information unrelated to his book. The SEC maintains that the employee misappropriated data for over 700,000 client accounts and then transferred the data over the

143

internet to his personal server. The SEC accuses the respondent firm with violating Regulation S-P's Safeguards Rule because its policies and procedures failed to properly restrict access, ensure auditing/testing of their effectiveness, and monitor employee access.

The SEC appears to impose a strict liability standard on cybersecurity breaches. Although it appears that the firm had significant cybersecurity policies in place, the fact that an employee was able to hack the system to misappropriate customer information makes it difficult to argue that those policies and procedures were reasonable.

BD Fined for Hack of Third Party Cloud Provider (*In re Lincoln Financial Securities*; 11/16/16)

A broker-dealer agreed to pay a $650,000 fine because an OSJ's cloud server vendor failed to protect customer information. FINRA asserts that foreign hackers penetrated the cloud-based servers and had access to customers' nonpublic personal information. FINRA faults the firm for failing to monitor or test the third party vendor's information security. FINRA also alleges that the BD failed to adopt reasonable data security policies that included specific firewall policies and related testing. FINRA cites violations of Rule 30 of Regulation S-P, which requires the protection of customer records and information.

Firms must go the extra mile to protect customer information and not just rely on hiring a third party. FINRA will hold BDs strictly liable for data breaches, even those occurring at the vendor.

Internet Company Pays $35 Million for Failing to Timely Disclose Hack of Customer Info (*In re Altaba (Yahoo)*; 4/25/18)

A large publicly traded internet media company agreed to pay a $35 Million fine and cooperate with investigators for failing to timely disclose a hacker breach of more than 500 million client accounts. The SEC charges that the respondent waited nearly 2 years before disclosing the breach, during which time it filed misleading annual reports and Form 10-Ks and

10-Qs. Additionally, the SEC accuses the company with filing a stock purchase agreement (as part of Form 8-K) that included misrepresentations about security breaches, thereby leading to a $350 Million reduction in the purchase price. A senior SEC official advised: "Public companies should have controls and procedures in place to properly evaluate cyber incidents and disclose material information to investors."

When it comes to cybersecurity incidents, time is not on your side. Because of the potential harm to clients and investors, it is better to provide immediate disclosure that will be followed up with additional information rather than waiting and thereby compounding the potential harm. Hacked firms must move quickly to investigate, assess, and remediate the harm to minimize damages.

SEC Warns Firms to Take Action Against Cyber-Frauds (10/18/18)

The SEC has issued an investigative report that advises public companies to enhance internal accounting controls to prevent losses from cyber-related frauds. The SEC report describes frauds at 9 issuers that involved spoofing emails and false vendor invoices that resulted in significant losses when internal employees transferred funds to the wrongdoers. One of the companies made 14 wire payments, resulting in a loss of over $45 Million. Another paid 8 invoices totaling $1.5 Million. Although the SEC did not bring enforcement actions against these registrants, the SEC alleges that the companies violated their obligations to implement internal accounting controls sufficient to ensure transactions are only permitted with management's authorization. In particular, the SEC advises companies to review and enhance their payment authorization and verification procedures and employee training. SEC Chairman Jay Clayton warned: "Cyber frauds are a pervasive, significant, and growing threat to all companies, including our public companies."

You've been warned. The SEC gave these 9 companies a pass, but we don't expect the same treatment for future violators who should now take action to prevent spoofing and email cyber-frauds.

D. <u>The States and FINRA</u>. Both the states and FINRA have brought cases alleging failures to protect data.

Large Insurance Company Settles for $5.5 Million over Data Breach (*In re Nationwide*; 8/16/17)

A large insurance company agreed to pay a total of $5.5 Million to settle charges brought by 32 states resulting from the loss of critical consumer information attributable to a criminal data breach. According to the Settlement Agreement, the respondent lost the data for 1.27 million customers across the country when hackers exploited a security breach created when the respondent failed to implement a security patch. As part of the settlement, the insurance company agreed to appoint a security patch supervisor, implement security patch policies and procedures, and perform internal assessments. The New York State Attorney General criticized the respondent for its their "true carelessness while collecting and retaining information from prospective customers, needlessly exposing their personal data in the process." He warned, "This settlement should serve as a reminder that companies have a responsibility to protect consumers' personal information regardless of whether or not those consumers become customers. We will hold companies to account if they don't."

The NYS Attorney General implies that companies can be held liable for data breaches that result from simple negligence rather than recklessness or intent. A solid compliance program that includes a robust cybersecurity assessment can help defend charges that a firm acted negligently.

NYS Attorney General Reports 1500 Data Breaches in 2017 (4/12/18)

The New York State Attorney General has issued a report indicating that a record 1583 data breaches affecting 9.2 million New Yorkers were reported to the NYAG in 2017. The information exposed included social security numbers (40%) and financial account information (33%). Hacking was the leading cause of the data security breaches. NYAG Eric Schneiderman warned "My office will continue to hold companies accountable for protecting the personal information they manage." The NYAG has urged the New York State legislature to pass the SHIELD Act, which would require companies to adopt reasonable safeguards to protect sensitive data, including relevant policies and procedures.

The state regulators have taken a primary role in enforcing data protection safeguards. Make sure your compliance procedures have the necessary policies and procedures that include governance, incident response, vulnerability assessment, and vendor management.

FINRA Posts Social Media and Digital Content Guidance (5/10/17)

FINRA has published a Regulatory Notice that provides guidance on the content, recordkeeping, and supervision of certain digital communications. FINRA clarifies that text and chat messages with clients must be retained as customer communications to the same extent as written or email communications. FINRA also offers guidance on when broker-dealers adopt or become entangled when using hyperlinks and other third party content. Sharing content through hyperlink will make a firm responsible for the third party content unless the third party site is dynamic, ongoing, and not influenced by the firm. However, a firm may not use a link to a third party that the "firm knows or has reason to know contains false or misleading content." FINRA also offers guidance on the use of native advertising, mandating that such content disclose the firm's name, any relationship, and whether mentioned products or services are offered by the firm. FINRA will allow unsolicited third party opinions posted on social media sites (e.g. "likes" on Facebook) so long as a registered representative does not subsequently endorse the third party opinion. FINRA makes clear that the guidance does not change prior rules and does not interpret SEC rules that apply to advisers.

Give FINRA credit for its ongoing regulatory guidance that reflects evolving social media and digital content. The guidance on texts, chats and hyperlinks are fairly reasonable. The challenge for compliance officers is to find emerging technologies and systems to capture the emerging content.

E. <u>Criminal Penalties</u>. The Justice Department has brought criminal charges when electronic communications cross state lines.

Adviser Jailed for Fraud Based on Emails that Crossed State Lines (*In re Holt*; 4/17/17)

A financial adviser was sentenced to 10 years in prison and ordered to make $2.9 Million in restitution because his emails that furthered his activities were transmitted over state lines, thereby constituting federal wire fraud. The SEC alleged that the defendant used cross-border emails and a web-based portal to provide false account statements and Ponzi-like payments. The SEC asserts that he misappropriated client funds by stealing their checks and depositing them into his bank account. The U.S. Attorney brought a criminal indictment against him for wire fraud based on the emails.

Federal wire fraud crime carries big prison and financial penalties. In this case, the U.S. Attorney leveraged the SEC charges into a federal conviction based on his cross-state emails.

FIVE ACTION ITEMS:

1. Conduct an internal assessment of the location of confidential information and who might have access.

2. Restrict employees by requiring (i) unique and dynamic passwords that expire and (ii) the exclusive use of firm-approved, encrypted devices.

3. Ensure your IT department conducts penetration testing and practices intrusion monitoring.

4. Evaluate your vendors' security protocols and cybersecurity protections.

5. Create a realistic incident response plan that requires notices to clients and regulators as well as an explanation of how to patch vulnerabilities.

8

TREND

Product marketers are
re-assessing traditional
marketing, distribution, and
revenue sharing.

When the SEC examiners arrive, they often begin with a review of the firm's marketing and advertising materials. From the regulator's perspective, misleading marketing materials are the "canary in the coal mine" warning that the firm has a weak control and compliance infrastructure. Deceptive marketing materials also suggest that a firm's leadership does not exhibit the requisite compliance "tone at the top."

> " [M]isleading marketing materials are the "canary in the coal mine" warning that the firm has a weak control and compliance infrastructure. "

Advisers and broker-dealers utilizing marketing materials that inflate performance or credentials is not a new phenomenon. What makes this area a trend is the SEC's renewed focus. In September 2017, seemingly out of the blue, OCIE warned advisers about misleading marketing practices that were uncovered during 1,000 examinations. These included overstating performance (such as presenting performance gross of fees), touting undocumented GIPS compliance, and unlawfully using past specific recommendations. Apparently, a wide swath of advisers either forgot or never learned some of the marketing regulation basics. Several enforcement actions followed, including five actions against firms who unlawfully used client testimonials (*In re HBA Advisors et. al.*).

Misleading performance claims still represent the basis for the vast majority of deficiencies and enforcement actions in this area, even after years of precedent and SEC guidance. In fact, for much of the Advisers Act's history, the SEC completely outlawed the marketing of performance as inherently deceptive. Over the last thirty years, the SEC has loosened up a bit, but the rules remain extremely restrictive. In recent years, the SEC has expanded reviews to include performance claims made by third parties. In a series of cases, the SEC brought enforcement actions against at least seventeen advisers for marketing unverified performance claims made by F-Squared—claims that the SEC contends were unsubstantiated and inflated based on hypothetical, backtested data.

The SEC really dislikes the use of hypothetical and/or backtested performance. Although not illegal per se, the SEC will usually claim that the firm failed to include enough disclosure (or maintain sufficient backup data) to make hypothetical performance claims. In *Raymond J. Lucia et al.*, the radio host was accused of using false inflation rates and failing to show the effects of reallocations. We generally advise clients to completely refrain from using hypothetical and backtested performance. Regardless of our regulatory concerns, we have found that most institutional investors ignore hypothetical performance claims because they understand the limitations of investment "Monday morning quarterbacking."

The SEC has also taken firms to task for failing to fully disclose how they actually manage assets. An ongoing concern is the recommendation of proprietary products without full disclosure of fees and risks and without disclosing the availability of nonproprietary products. In *Citigroup*, the SEC accused the firm's financial advisers of characterizing their leverage-laden hedge funds as safe and liquid bond alternatives, even though the disclosure documents said otherwise. In *SEC v. Persaud*, the Enforcement Division accused the adviser of failing to inform clients that he based his investment decisions on astrological factors. The SEC has also charged advisers with failing to conduct the promised due diligence on underlying investments (*SEC v. Bekkedam*) and with neglecting to disclose coding errors in their quantitative trading models (*In re AXA Rosenberg*). Misleading performance claims could also relate to marketing statements about specific recommendations or a spotless regulatory record.

Ever since the regulatory separation of small advisers (regulated by the states) and larger advisers (regulated by the SEC), the SEC has increased its scrutiny of how firms market their total assets under management. The SEC has recognized that firms have an incentive to claim AUM above $100 Million— and thus SEC registration eligibility—because institutional investors usually weed out state-registered advisers from consideration for mandates. Not surprisingly, firms that are near this demarcation line can get creative with how they calculate AUM (see, e.g., *In re Black Diamond Asset Management; In re Bantry Bay Capital*). The SEC and the well-known firm of Dawn Bennett continue to litigate whether the firm's claims of $2 Billion in assets under management, which ensured higher rankings in national publications, can be substantiated (*In re Bennett Group*).

During the last couple of years, the SEC has also fixated on all forms of undisclosed revenue sharing. Many of these cases have involved mutual fund 12b-1 payments or shareholder servicing payments that the SEC asserts were nothing more than hidden distribution fees paid by clients. (*see, e.g., In re First Eagle Investment Management; In re William Blair & Company; In re Calvert*). On the other side of the transaction, the SEC has brought many cases against advisers who failed to fully disclose revenue sharing received from product sponsors (*see, e.g., In re Voya Financial*). The SEC has also faulted firms that failed to fully disclose a wide range of wrongful practices that resulted in the adviser receiving undisclosed compensation: hidden fees, undisclosed commissions, inflated valuations, proprietary products, and mark-ups.

Fortunately, investment management professionals should be able to sidestep regulatory challenges by reviewing the long history of rules, guidance, and enforcement actions relating to marketing and advertising. The black letter rules are fairly easy to follow: Present actual performance net of fees. Do not use past specific recommendations. Don't use testimonials. Don't claim you have some sort of "black box" trading methodology that works for everybody. And, most importantly, don't lie to your clients or prospects!

A. <u>OCIE Alert</u>. OCIE issued an alert on common marketing and advertising deficiencies uncovered during exams.

SEC Warns Advisers about Misleading Advertising Practices (9/18/17)

The SEC's Office of Compliance Inspections and Examinations has issued a Risk Alert citing common investment adviser marketing and advertising compliance issues. OCIE, drawing on over 1000 examinations and its recent "Touting Initiative," cited several deficiencies: (i) misleading performance results including failure to present performance net of fees, comparisons to inapplicable benchmarks, and hypothetical/back-tested performance, (ii) misleading claims about compliance with voluntary performance standards (i.e. CFA Institute), and (iii) cherry-picked performance and misleading presentations of past specific recommendations. The SEC also criticized advertising that cited third party awards or rankings without proper explanation. The SEC urges advisers to "assess the full scope of their advertisements and consider whether those advertisements are consistent with the Advertising Rule, the prohibitions of Section 206, and their fiduciary duties, and review the adequacy and effectiveness of their compliance programs."

OCIE generally issues these types of Risk Alerts in advance of bringing enforcement actions. Although the SEC has not generally brought enforcement cases solely on the basis of misleading performance claims, this Risk Alert may signal a change in enforcement policy.

SEC Charges Violations of Testimonial Rule (*In re HBA Advisors, et. al.*; 7/12/18)

The SEC settled five enforcement actions against two investment advisers, three investment adviser representatives, and the principal of a third-party marketing firm for utilizing the internet to disseminate unlawful client testimonials. Three of the actions involved a testimonial program sold by the third-party marketing firm that solicited client testimonials for publication on social media websites. Clients lauded the subject firms for service, returns, knowledge, and market access. One of the firms sought positive reviews on Yelp that it would endorse. One of the firms posted client videos on YouTube. The SEC charged the principal of the third-party marketing firm with causing his client's violations. The testimonial rule (206(4)-1(a)(1)) prohibits advertisements that refer to any testimonial about advice, analysis, or services.

Last September, OCIE warned advisers against misleading marketing practices. It's hard to believe that advisers could violate the testimonial rule, a clear prohibition that has been in effect for decades. If you don't know the rules, hire a compli-pro to ensure you don't violate the black letter rules.

Court Enters Judgment against Fund Adviser for Resume Inflation (*SEC v. Moses*; 2/12/18)

The United States District Court for the District of Colorado entered a default judgment against a state-registered fund manager for misrepresenting his experience and credentials, among other false statements. As part of his fund-raising efforts, the fund manager claimed to have extensive portfolio management experience including successful management of several large private funds. The SEC alleges that, although the defendant worked for the organizations referenced, he never served as a portfolio manager and generally acted in minor consulting roles unrelated to portfolio management. Additionally, the SEC charges that the defendant made unsubstantiated performance claims.

When you engage in resume inflation to raise money, you have engaged in securities fraud. You also run the risk of a criminal prosecution under 10b-5.

SEC Charges Adviser with Lying about SEC Deficiencies in RFPs (5/10/11; *In re Aletheia*)

The SEC has fined and imposed disclosure obligations on an RIA that failed to disclose SEC deficiencies in RFPs. The SEC alleges that the RIA responded to at least 10 RFPs for institutional mandates that requested information about deficiencies in SEC exams. According to the SEC, the respondent and its two principals ignored the question, answered with respect to a related entity, or indicated that "there were no significant findings." The SEC notes that a 2005 exam resulted in a 7-page deficiency letter. The SEC also charges the firm's CCO for aiding and abetting violations of Rule 206(4)-7 because he had knowledge of the exam deficiencies and participated in the RFP process. In addition to fines against the firm and the principals, the SEC settlement requires the firm to retain an independent consultant and disclose the action in its ADV and on its website.

The SEC will review RFP responses during an exam. Questions about SEC exam deficiencies are fairly common. Firms will not win the argument that a particular deficiency was not "material" or "significant."

B. <u>Misleading Performance Claims</u>. The SEC will prosecute firms for touting misleading performance, especially when based on hypothetical and/or backtested data.

Manager-of-Managers Will Pay $16.5 Million for Failing to Verify Performance (*In re Virtus*; 11/17/15)

A fund manager and adviser agreed to pay $16.5 Million in fines, disgorgement, and interest, for failing to verify performance information provided by a subadviser. According to the SEC, the respondent advertised actual performance that was instead based on unsubstantiated backtested and hypothetical performance data. The SEC charges the firm with failing to adopt compliance policies and procedures "for evaluating and monitoring the accuracy of third-party-produced performance information" and failing to maintain sufficient books and records to support performance claims. The SEC also faults the firm for ignoring red flags including concerns raise by FINRA and a data provider.

What compliance procedures must a manager-of-managers implement to ensure performance claims made by third parties? Should it conduct a forensic review of all underlying performance data to ensure accurate performance reporting? To satisfy the books and records requirement, must a firm require a dump of all supporting data? Does this case raise the bar for managers-of-managers who are not permitted to rely on information provided by third-party managers?[23]

SEC ALJ Holds that Claims of GIPS Compliance are Material and Investor Reliance is not Required (*In re ZPR Investment Management;* 6/2/14)

An SEC Administrative Law Judge has ruled that misleading claims of GIPS compliance are material and that the SEC need not prove that an investor actually relied on the misleading statements. The case at issue involved allegedly misleading claims of GIPS compliance in advertising materials. The respondent argued that the materials were not misleading because all of the numbers were accurate. The ALJ opined that the false claims of GIPS compliance made the materials misleading because institutional investors consider GIPS compliance claims when making investment decisions. The ALJ also indicated that the SEC does not have the same burden of proof as securities fraud private litigants who must show actual reliance on misleading statements. The ALJ also made clear that reprints of investment report newsletters are deemed "advertisements".

When reviewing marketing and advertising materials, firms should review every sentence for accuracy and then review the totality of the piece to ensure that the document as a whole is not misleading even if every sentence is accurate. The SEC will presume materiality of any statement a firm includes in its marketing and advertising.

---

23 The *Virtus* case suggests that a firm must conduct additional due diligence on third party products that claim significant outperformance.

Adviser Marketed Misleading Hypothetical Backtested Performance (*In re Arlington Capital Management*; 4/18/18)

The SEC censured and fined an investment adviser and its principal for misleading advertisements that utilized hypothetical backtested performance. According to the SEC, the adviser continually updated its models but failed to fully disclose that the models' out-performance resulted from these post hoc revisions. The SEC alleges that the respondents revised the models to specifically account for unforeseen events such as market movements. The SEC charges the firm and the principal, who also acted as the Chief Compliance Officer, with engaging in manipulative practices and for failing to implement a reasonable compliance program. As part of the settlement, the firm agreed to retain a dedicated Chief Compliance Officer and an outside compliance consultant.

As we have advised many times in the past: (i) do not advertise hypothetical backtested performance and (ii) retain a dedicated Chief Compliance Officer that has regulatory credentials. Also, rather than continue to bring these cases whereby a dual-hatted principal continues to fail as Chief Compliance Officer, the SEC should solve this pandemic by requiring all advisers to undergo periodic third party compliance reviews.

SEC Prosecutes Radio Host for Using Misleading Backtested Performance (*In re Raymond J. Lucia*; 9/17/12)

The SEC instituted an enforcement proceeding against a syndicated radio host for false performance claims based on unsupported backtesting.[24] The SEC described how the respondent marketed his various strategies by claiming that returns were backtested over several decades. The SEC charges that the respondent did not have sufficient supporting documentation. Moreover, the SEC alleges that the respondent utilized hypothetical inflation rates and REIT return rates that benefited the purported results, even though actual data was readily available. Also,

---

24   Lucia was barred and fined $300,000. Following appeal, the Supreme Court ruled that the ALJ that decided the case was not properly appointed. The SEC may choose to retry the case in front of a new ALJ.

the SEC alleges that the respondent failed to show the negative effects of re-allocations during the backtested periods. The SEC charges violations of the Adviser Act's antifraud rules and the marketing rule.

Avoid using backtested performance data. Although the SEC has no rule specifically outlawing the practice, the burden of proof is very high (perhaps impossibly high) to prove that you have not misled investors.

Investment Newsletter Violated Rule Prohibiting Past Specific Recommendations (*In re Stock Markets Institute*; 9/24/12)

An investment newsletter publisher agreed to fines and sanctions (including the appointment of an independent compliance consultant) for violating the SEC's prohibition on advertising past specific recommendations. According to the SEC, the respondents claimed significant success with its recommended options strategy, including 100% successful trades over two years. However, the SEC charges that the respondents failed to include losing options trades that were rolled into new positions to avoid realizing a loss. The respondent also recorded one successful recommendation as several when executed through multiple brokers. The SEC charges that the respondents violated Rule 206(4)-1(a)(5), which prohibits the use of past specific recommendations unless all recommendations made in the prior year are included.

Many firms struggle with the prohibition against publishing past specific recommendations. It is a strict liability rule in that firms must include 12 months of recommendations whether or not the few they would otherwise choose demonstrate good or bad performance.

C. <u>Misrepresenting Investments</u>. Fund managers and advisers must not misrepresent how investments are managed.

Hedge Fund Sponsor to Pay $180 Million to Settle Misrepresentation Charges (*In re Citigroup*; 8/18/15)

A large hedge fund sponsor agreed to pay $180 Million in restitution and interest for recommending proprietary hedge funds that collapsed during the financial crisis. According to the SEC, affiliated financial advisers and the fund manager described the funds, which employed significant leverage, as safe, liquid, bond alternatives. The oral communications contradicted statements made in written disclosure documents. The respondents continued to sell the funds even as they experienced significant financial deterioration in 2007. The SEC charges violations of the anti-fraud rules as well as the compliance rule (206(4)-7) for failing to implement policies and procedures to supervise oral sales communications. Andrew Ceresney, Director of the SEC's Enforcement Division, said "Firms cannot insulate themselves from liability for their employees' misrepresentations by invoking the fine print contained in written disclosures."

Compliance policies must include procedures to make sure that sales representatives don't contradict the written offering documents. These procedures could include approval of presentations, listening to recorded conversations, training, and supervisory participation in sales meetings.

SEC Bars Adviser Who Failed to Disclose Astrology-Based Investment Strategy (*SEC v. Persaud*; 5/15/14))

The SEC barred from the industry an investment adviser that it alleges failed to disclose that he based his strategy on the lunar cycles and the "gravitational pull between the Earth and the moon." The SEC charges that the defendant hid trading losses by delivering false client statements. The SEC also faults the adviser with making misrepresentations about guaranteed returns and safety of assets and misappropriating client funds.

It is very important to fully disclose the investment style utilized to manage client assets.

SEC Sues Adviser Principal for Failing to Conduct Due Diligence (*SEC v. Bekkedam*; 5/2/14)

The SEC has commenced securities fraud proceedings against an RIA's principal for failing to conduct the promised due diligence on an investment that turned out to be a Ponzi scheme.[25] The SEC states that the PPM and the LPA for the subject fund included disclosure about the significant due diligence performed by the adviser and the information available to the adviser. However, the SEC alleges, that the adviser did not conduct the due diligence or obtain the information. Although the adviser repeatedly failed in his attempts to obtain information and conduct due diligence, he continued to solicit investors for the fund. The SEC cites emails where the defendant expresses his frustration with the fund sponsor and the underlying investment. The SEC states that the defendant had a duty to disclose the material misstatements and omissions in the PPM "in connection with the positive statements regarding that investment and recommendation" that clients invest in the fund.

What are the due diligence of obligations of a registered investment adviser? It is not entirely clear. However, an adviser must at least conduct the due diligence that it says it will do. Also, an adviser should avoid making any positive statements about a fund investment lest the adviser be held accountable for all statements made in the PPM.

Faulty Computer Coding and Inadequate Compliance Blamed for $200 Million Client Losses (2/7/11; *In re AXA Rosenberg*)

A large institutional quant manager has agreed to pay over $200 Million and overhaul its compliance infrastructure in response to SEC charges that it failed to disclose errors in its quantitative trading model. The SEC alleges that the firm knew about coding errors that affected risk management procedures within the system but failed to take action for several months. The SEC also alleges that the firm's compliance policies and procedures did not include quality control testing over the coding process and did not sufficiently identify and mitigate the risks associated with the quantitative model's development, testing, and change control procedures. The SEC also charges that the firm violated its compliance policies because known issues were not properly escalated within the firm.

---

25 The principal was sentenced to eleven months in prison on unrelated bank fraud charges.

Most compliance manuals focus primarily on regulatory risk. In this case, the SEC states that a firm's policies and procedures must also address operational risk such as computer coding, which if written incorrectly, could cause a firm to make misrepresentations to clients.

Large Asset Manager Pays $97 Million for Over-Relying on Faulty Quant Models (*In re Aegon USA*; 8/28/18)

A large asset manager agreed to pay over $97 Million in disgorgement, fines and interest for over-relying on and marketing faulty quantitative models and other portfolio management missteps. The SEC maintains that the respondents rolled out registered funds and separate accounts based on untested quantitative models created by an inexperienced research analyst. When the models failed to work as described to the Board and investors, the respondents discontinued their use without explanation or disclosure. The SEC also accuses the firm of declaring dividends without proper disclosure of the percentage attributable to return of capital and for using third party performance data without verification. The SEC charges violations of the anti-fraud rules, the compliance rule, and Section 15(c) of the Investment Company Act for lying to the funds' Board.

This case reads like a cautionary tale for large firms trying to quickly roll out a product. It appears that the portfolio management, marketing, legal, operations, and legal functions worked in silos, and, as a result, failed to properly vet or describe the products. We recommend that firms create a cross-functional product assessment team that can ask the hard questions before launching a product.

D. Inflating AUM. Don't inflate assets under management to claim registration eligibility.

Adviser Accused of Stretching the Truth on AUM Calculation (*In re Bennett Group*; 9/11/15)

The SEC has commenced enforcement proceedings against an investment adviser for inflating assets under management and investment returns and then lying to SEC Enforcement investigators about how it arrived at the inflated AUM figure.[26] According to the SEC, the respondent claimed over $2 Billion in AUM so that it could be highly ranked in *Barron's* and then used its ranking for marketing. The respondent also touted the AUM in a radio show. To substantiate the claims, the respondent claimed that the firm managed cash of three companies with which the principal had a relationship. The SEC could not verify any significant advisory relationship after contacting the purported clients. The SEC argues that the "[i]nformal and uncompensated conversations about what entities might want to do with assets (which are not held in any account serviced by the brokerage or advisory firm) cannot meaningfully be described as the management of those assets."

While the calculation of AUM can be subjective, firms should not count uncompensated assets and undocumented services for assets held outside any brokerage account related to the adviser. Also, advisers must understand that private statements or responses made with the understanding that the recipient will disseminate that information constitute advertisements under the Advisers Act. Finally, don't lie to SEC Enforcement investigators.

SEC Accuses Adviser of Falsely Inflating AUM to Register (*In re Black Diamond Asset Management*; 8/7/17)

The SEC instituted enforcement proceedings against an adviser that it accuses of falsely claiming SEC registration eligibility. The SEC alleges that the adviser initially registered by claiming that it had over $500 Million in assets under management and a year later changed its ADV to claim eligibility as a mid-sized adviser ($25-$100 Million AUM) domiciled in New York and/or Wyoming. However, the SEC maintains that the adviser never had any clients or assets under management. The SEC further accuses the adviser of soliciting clients using the false ADVs.

SEC registration has become a qualifying criterion for larger clients who feel more secure with an SEC-regulated firm that has more than

---

26   As of this writing, the litigation continues.

$100 Million in AUM. Consequently, firms may feel the pressure to stretch their numbers to qualify, which could result in a painful enforcement action. There is no shortcut to success.

Adviser's Form ADV Inflated Assets to Claim SEC Registration Eligibility (*In re Bantry Bay Capital*; 7/3/17)

An investment adviser was fined and barred from the industry for falsely claiming SEC registration eligibility, along with several other Advisers Act violations. The SEC asserts that the respondent filed multiple Form ADVs claiming over $100 Million in AUM and SEC registration eligibility even though the firm had only $4 Million in AUM. The SEC also charges the firm with misappropriating client assets, failing to comply with the custody and recordkeeping rules, and charging excessive fees.

Whether to register with the SEC or the relevant state is not a discretionary decision. Either you have $100 Million in AUM or you don't. Lying on a Form ADV about SEC registration eligibility will result in a public enforcement action, censure and fines.

❑ *The List: Ten Most Significant Form ADV Changes*

Ten Most Significant Form ADV Changes

1.	**Separately Managed Accounts.** The new Form ADV requires significant reporting on separately managed account assets including reporting by asset type and related derivative transactions.
2.	**Umbrella Registration.** The new filing rules allow affiliated advisers to use a single ADV, but the registrant must complete a detailed schedule for each relying adviser
3.	**Social Media.** Every registrant must include websites and social media addresses.
4.	**Offices.** An adviser with multiple offices must list its largest 25 offices (used to be 5).
5.	**Outside CCO.** If a firm retains a Chief Compliance Officer paid by a third party, the new Form requires the registrant to name the CCO and his/her employer.

6.	**Assets Under Management.** The new Form ADV requires more detailed reporting of regulatory assets under management by client type.
7.	**Wrap Programs.** Registrants must include more detailed information about the wrap programs in which they participate.
8.	**Referral Payments.** The new rules require more disclosure about compensation paid or received for referrals including amounts paid by, or to, employees.
9.	**Bad Actors.** The bad actor disclosure (DRP) requires information about all relying advisers.
10.	**Auditors.** The new Form ADV requires information about the auditors to private funds.

E. <u>Distribution-in-Guise</u>. The SEC has brought many cases alleging "distribution-in-guise" for the payment of revenue sharing by mutual funds.

Fund Sponsor to Pay $40 Million for Using Fund Assets to Pay for Distribution (*In re First Eagle Investment Management*; 9/22/15)

A mutual fund sponsor agreed to pay $40 Million in disgorgement, fines, and interest for using fund assets to pay for distribution services without approval by the Board or shareholders. The SEC charges the respondent with mischaracterizing distribution payments as sub-Transfer Agent services such as recordkeeping and other shareholder servicing. Instead, the Agreements with two broker-dealers specifically required payment for distribution and marketing services based on a percentage of assets sold. The SEC indicates that such payments could only be made out of the adviser's assets or pursuant to a 12b-1 plan approved by the Board and shareholders. The SEC charges the respondent with making misleading statements to both the Board and to shareholders in the prospectus. The SEC has indicated that this is the first case brought under its Distribution-in-Guise Initiative that seeks "to determine whether some mutual fund advisers are improperly using fund assets to pay for distribution by masking the payments as subtransfer agency (subTA) payments."

From an SEC enforcement perspective, this was a "good" set of facts because the intermediary agreements specifically said that the payments were for distribution. The more difficult question is whether the SEC will seek to re-characterize documented shareholder servicing or sub-TA payments as disguised distribution payments based on a calculation of benefits derived or actual activities undertaken.

Fund Company Fined $4.5 Million for Unlawful Distribution-in-Guise (*In re William Blair & Company*; 5/3/17)

A mutual fund manager agreed to pay a $4.5 Million fine and reimburse the funds another $1.25 Million for making unlawful distribution and sub-transfer agency payments to intermediaries. The SEC maintains that the fund company claimed to make payments solely out of its revenues but, as a result of a technical misclassification, paid amounts directly out of fund assets in violation of Rule 12b-1. The SEC also asserts that the respondent paid sub-TA fees in excess of Board-approved caps disclosed in the registration statement. The SEC charges violations of the antifraud provisions of the Advisers Act and the Investment Company Act (Sections 206(2) and 34(b), respectively) and Section 12(b) and Rule 12b-1 of the Investment Company Act for making distribution payments without proper Board and shareholder approval and disclosure.

This the SEC's second major case pursuant to its distribution-in-guise initiative (See Fund Sponsor to Pay $40 Million for Using Fund Assets to Pay for Distribution). Fund firms must make sure that sub-TA payments do not include payments for any kind of distribution or marketing services. Also, Boards must vet and approve all such plans that make use of fund assets.

Another Mutual Fund Firm Fined for Distribution-In-Guise (*In re Calvert*; 5/4/17)

Another mutual fund manager was censured and penalized ($22.6 Million) for paying distribution and marketing fees mischaracterized as sub-TA fees, in violation of Section 12(b) and Rule 12b-1 of the Investment Company Act. The SEC alleges that the fund sponsor, through the manager and distributor, used fund assets to pay for distribution but told intermediaries and the Board that such amounts were for sub-TA (shareholder) services and would be paid out of the manager's revenue rather than fund assets. Additionally, the SEC charges that, even if the amounts were paid for legitimate sub-TA services, such amounts exceeded the caps set by agreements with the funds.

Many in the fund industry were waiting for the regulatory shoe to drop after the SEC first announced the distribution-in-guise sweep two years ago. This makes 2 cases in 2 days against large fund companies. Compliance officers must do their own sweep to determine whether fund sponsors are properly compensating intermediaries.

SEC Staff Demands Heightened Board Scrutiny of Servicing Fees (1/7/16)

The staff of the SEC's Division of Investment Management has issued guidance advising Boards and fund managers how to assess the permissibility of fees paid to intermediaries. The staff requires the Board to determine whether payments made to intermediaries (as sub-transfer agent, administrative, sub-accounting, or similarly-categorized shareholder servicing fees) are disguised distribution payments only permissible pursuant to shareholder-approved 12b-1 distribution plans. The staff requires the fund's adviser and other service providers to provide the Board with sufficient information to make such determinations. The staff outlines the information that the Board should receive including services rendered, amounts paid, fee structures, and reasonableness. The staff also highlights several practices that deserve heightened Board scrutiny including distribution activity conditioned on receipt of fees, the absence of a 12b-1 plan, tiered payment structures, bundling of services, and large disparities in fees paid to different third-party providers. The staff also recommends that funds adopt compliance policies and procedures to review and identify payments that may be made for distribution-related services.

Boards should consider adding a distribution review similar to the advisory contract review process, whereby the Adviser must deliver significant information for the Board to deliberately consider any

shareholder servicing payment according to the staff's guidance. Fund CCOs need to get working on policies and procedures and testing protocols.

F. <u>Undisclosed Compensation</u>. The SEC has closely scrutinized other forms of undisclosed compensation including various forms of revenue sharing.

Large Adviser Penalized $3 Million over Revenue Sharing (*In re Voya Financial*; 3/10/17)

A large investment adviser agreed to pay over $3 Million in disgorgement, fines and interest for failing to disclose mutual fund revenue sharing received from its clearing broker. The SEC alleges that, during the last 10 years, the clearing broker paid the adviser a portion of trailer fees received from mutual funds to which the adviser directed client assets. The SEC also described an arrangement whereby the clearing broker paid the adviser for certain shareholder services. The SEC faults the adviser for failing to disclose in either the ADV or its client agreements that it received payments and that such payments created a conflict of interest. The adviser and clearing broker have since altered their agreement so that the revenue sharing is calculated based on total assets rather than the funds in which the adviser invests client assets.

The SEC does not allege that this conflict actually harmed any client, or that the revenue sharing had any empirical effect on the adviser's investment decisions. Also, the SEC seems to be ok with revenue sharing that does not present a potential conflict of interest i.e. based on total assets. It is also less than clear whether disclosure would have actually cured the SEC's conflict of interest concerns.

Longstanding Church Fund Violated Fiduciary Duty (*In re Institutional Investors Advisory Company*; 8/21/17)

The sponsor of a church fund agreed to pay over $2.25 Million in returned profits, disgorgement, interest and penalties for failing to properly disclose a reserve fund created to smooth returns. According to the SEC, the Board of the fund, which was launched in 1973, created the reserve fund in 1993 as a vehicle to retain excess profits and ensure liquidity so that the fund could distribute consistent returns between 5% and 6.7%. The SEC faults the fund sponsor for failing to fully disclose that it would charge fees on the reserve fund and that redeeming investors would not receive their pro rata amounts held in the reserve fund. OCIE identified the fiduciary violations during a 2014 exam, which followed the sponsor's registration in 2012.

The SEC appears to be most disturbed that the fund sponsor did not return client assets and double-dipped advisory fees by moving assets into the reserve fund. Private fund firms that registered after 2012 as a result of Dodd-Frank, should audit their operations to determine whether longstanding business practices run afoul of their fiduciary duties.

Large Custody Bank to Pay $32 Million for Undisclosed Transition Management Compensation (*In re State Street Global Markets*; 9/8/17)

A large custody bank agreed to pay $32.3 Million to settle allegations that it charged undisclosed commissions and mark-ups as part of its transition management services to large plans and sovereign wealth funds. According to the SEC, the respondent's scheme involved bidding for transition management projects with artificially low commission schedules and then charging undisclosed mark-ups and concealing those mark-ups when reporting to clients. The SEC's investigation included emails and recorded conversations where internal employees (i) referred to such concealed mark-ups as a "rounding error," (ii) committed to "make it work" internally when forced to bid at low commission rates, (iii) bragged that they would "back the truck up" when describing the undisclosed commissions, and (iv) vowed that "This can of works stays closed" when discussing their scheme. A client's consultant ultimately discovered the undisclosed commissions.

You do know that your emails are retained and your conversations are recorded? Right? The bad old ways of hoping you won't get caught just have no place in the modern regulatory world where compliance officers, clients (and their consultants), and regulators all review sales activity and disclosure.

Fund Manager Used Spurious Matching Trades to Avoid Realized Losses (*SEC v. Hope Advisors*; 6/22/16)

The SEC has commenced enforcement proceedings against a fund manager and options trader for using non-economic options trades to defer realized losses while collecting incentive fees on realized gains. The SEC asserts that the respondent used matching options trades that had no economic purpose to indefinitely defer unrealized options losses because the calculation of the incentive fee only depended on realized losses and gains. Although aggregate unrealized losses accumulated over time, the respondent continued to collect management fees above the funds' high water marks based on realized gains. A foundation controlled by the principal is named as a relief defendant for having received unlawful contributions.

As a fiduciary, a fund manager cannot execute transactions that have no economic purpose other than to benefit the manager. Also, fund managers should not get overly-technical trying to interpret high water mark and incentive fee language in a manner that contradicts how investors would commonly interpret such provisions.

Hedge Fund Firm Pays Over $10 Million for Allowing PMs to Use Sham Broker Quotes (*In re Visium Asset Management*; 5/9/18)

A hedge fund firm agreed to pay over $10 Million in fines, disgorgement, and interest for failing to stop two portfolio managers from using sham broker quotes in a scheme to inflate fund NAVs. The SEC faults the firm for failing to observe its own valuation procedures by allowing the PMs significant influence to override pricing services, failing to conduct adequate due diligence of the brokers, and neglecting to obtain at least 3 broker quotes for a price override. The SEC also fined and barred the firm's CFO for failure to supervise by ignoring red flags such as the frequency that the PMs overrode prices and that overrides almost always resulted in higher valuations. The SEC previously charged the portfolio managers.

Investment firms and supervisors cannot turn a blind eye to questionable valuations and performance. According to the SEC, the respondent collected over $3 Million in unearned performance and management fees, making the firm ultimately responsible for its employees' wrongdoing.

SEC Sues Fund Portfolio Manager for Arranging Sham Broker Quotes (*SEC v. Lumiere*; 6/21/16)

The SEC commenced enforcement proceedings against a portfolio manager for arranging sham broker quotes to inflate securities valuations and NAV, thereby collecting higher management fees.[27] The SEC charges that the respondent fed sham quotes to friendly brokers that did business with the firm and then presented the fake quotes to the administrator as legitimate pricing sources to override administrator valuations. According to the SEC, over a 2-year period, the unlawful activity resulted in 7%-35% securities overvaluations, an overstatement of month-end NAV by as much as 7%, positive instead of negative fund performance, and $5 Million of ill-gotten management fees. The SEC asserts that the bogus valuation process conflicted with the firm's compliance manual, which the firm delivered to investors. The respondent also faces criminal charges.

The lesson for compli-pros and other risk managers is that an individual with an inherent conflict of interest will go to great lengths to line his/her pockets and hide the activity. Separately, we think it is a bad idea to deliver the compliance manual to clients because, as this case shows, the compliance manual can become the basis for a securities fraud claim.

RIA/BD Failed to Disclose Mark-Ups and 12b-1 Fees (*SEC v. Westport Capital Markets*; 12/13/17)

The SEC has commenced enforcement proceedings against a dually registered adviser/broker-dealer and its CEO/CCO principal for taking undisclosed commissions and 12b-1 fees on discretionary accounts. The SEC's complaint avers that the respondent sold inventory securities, acquired at a discount as part of the selling syndicate, to clients at a mark-up. The SEC alleges that the firm never obtained the required informed consent. The SEC also charges the firm for taking mutual fund 12b-1 fees without telling clients.

---

27   Lumiere was sentenced to eighteen months in prison and a $1 Million fine.

A principal transaction with a client requires an adviser fiduciary to obtain specific client consent following disclosure of all relevant information. The SEC continues its crackdown on any form of revenue sharing received by advisers with respect to their fiduciary clients.

Executing Broker to Pay $22.6 Million for Misrepresenting Order Filling Process (*In re Citadel Securities*; 1/24/17)

A large executing broker agreed to pay $22.6 Million to settle charges that it misled broker-dealers clients about the mechanism for filling orders. The SEC charges that the executing broker claimed that it would deliver best price but, instead, used two algorithms that capitalized on price discrepancies that often benefitted the respondent. An SEC official warned, "We are focused on the execution of retail orders and encourage investors to ask brokers, and brokers to ask internalizers, how they are determining best prices for retail orders."

This case looks like a disconnect between the front office and the back office. It appears that the folks talking to clients did not understand how the firm actually filled orders. "Don't let the facts ruin a good story" is a recipe for an enforcement action.

FIVE ACTION ITEMS:

1. Look at marketing materials like a regulator, not like a salesperson. Don't use absolute adjectives ("best," "largest," "oldest") and do define all the investment jargon ("standard deviation," "beta," "Black-Scholes").

2. If you need more than two sentences of disclosure, don't make the claim. Wordy disclosure is a red flag for the regulators and for institutional investors.

3. Review the materials prepared by your (large) competitors. Many lawyers and compli-pros understand the SEC's tolerance. Don't try to break new ground.

4. Review your materials for outlier performance claims. The capital markets are fairly efficient. Nobody beats benchmarks by several hundred basis points, unless they are misrepresenting their performance or using the wrong benchmarks.

5. Ensure your back office retains all the documentation necessary to recreate performance claims.

TREND

Whistleblowers are encouraged to snitch on their employers and competitors.

The SEC has awarded over $300 Million to more than fifty whistleblowers under the program established in 2011 to encourage insiders to report securities law violations. Modeled on the Sarbanes-Oxley whistleblower provisions, the Dodd-Frank whistleblower statute allows the SEC to award whistleblowers 10 percent to 30 percent of monetary sanctions if the sanctions imposed exceed $1 Million. In one recent example, a corporate officer who initially reported internally received a mid-six-figure whistleblower award following the 120-day period during which the company ignored his concerns. In another case, the SEC awarded a reporting compliance officer over $1 Million after the company failed to take steps to remedy the alleged misconduct.

The SEC claims to have imposed sanctions exceeding $1.7 billion based on whistleblower information. Whistleblower claims have accelerated exponentially over the last few years as the industry adjusts and the SEC's Office of the Whistleblower grows.

> " The SEC claims to have imposed sanctions exceeding $1.7 billion based on whistleblower information. "

The SEC whistleblower program has changed the financial industry. Investment firms must create an up-the-chain procedure to provide for the internal reporting of potential securities law violations. They must also create employment procedures that ensure the firm does not retaliate against whistleblowers. They must strike language from employment and severance agreements that would restrict a whistleblower from coming forward. Because the SEC has deputized every employee, investment firms must re-consider who has access to information and when to include outside counsel to ensure privilege. Rather than solve problems, disgruntled employees could use sensitive information to benefit themselves and harm the firm.

Potential whistleblowing employees must also change their behaviors. As described above, the SEC has targeted individuals who fail to stop internal wrongdoing. Now, an employee with knowledge of a possible securities law violations faces a difficult choice of doing nothing and incurring the SEC's wrath or reporting and thereby alienating the firm by becoming a whistleblower. The possibility of a whistleblower award down the road may be cold comfort.

Since the adoption of the program, the SEC has liberally interpreted whom it considers a potential whistleblower. Corporate officers, former employees, and even outsiders have received whistleblower awards. Compliance officers can also seek whistleblower protections so long as they give management notice and time to remedy the problem. An unintended consequence is that the compliance function may be denied access to sensitive information, which could have a counterproductive effect on the success of compliance programs.

The Supreme Court has limited the SEC by ruling that a potential whistleblower must report to the SEC, and not just internally, to benefit from the statute's protections (*Digital Realty Trust v. Somers*). The ruling makes the Dodd-Frank whistleblower program significantly different than its Sarbanes-Oxley ancestor. It also creates a bright-line test for companies and employees. Although we believe the Supreme Court made the right ruling based on the statute, we don't suspect Congress really intended to limit the program to SEC reporters. It is very possible that a future Congress may change the statute. Also, retaliation against internal reporters may still be protected by Sarbanes-Oxley and/or state law.

Following employment law precedent, the courts and the SEC have imposed significant penalties on firms that retaliate against whistleblowers, whether or not their claims were valid. Courts have assessed seven-figure-plus awards for wrongful termination or negative job actions. In *Wadler v. Bio-Rad*, a jury awarded a fired general counsel $7.9 Million for raising Foreign Corrupt Practices Act issues. The court rejected the company's argument that Wadler's information fell within attorney–client privilege. In *International Game Technology*, the SEC fined the company for retaliation even though the whistleblower was incorrect in his assertions that the company misstated its financial statements. In *Paradigm Capital Management*, the company mistakenly relied on the advice of employment counsel by marginalizing the whistleblower within the organization—resulting in a $2 Million restitution order.

The SEC has also imposed fines where employment or severance agreements have in any way limited the rights of employees to report wrongdoing. In *SandRidge Energy*, the SEC fined the oil and gas company $1.4 Million in part because its severance agreements restricted former employees from reporting to the SEC. Soon after OCIE issued a Risk Alert about agreements that restrict potential whistleblowers, the Enforcement Division fined Blackrock $340,000 because its severance agreements did not have specific language that excluded whistleblower activities, even though the SEC did not allege that the agreements actually impeded anybody.

Whistleblowers need not be corporate insiders, either. Hoping to attract the next Harry Markopolos, the SEC has awarded bounties to several third parties who have alleged wrongdoing, including one industry expert who conducted a detailed analysis as well as a former employee.

The potential pile of whistleblower cash has proven irresistible to many lawyers who previously made their careers out of pursuing securities law class actions. Because nearly anybody can be a whistleblower, these contingency lawyers solicit clients willing to serve as the aggrieved in exchange for a percentage of the potential award. The lawyer promises to handle all the filings and negotiations without charging a nickel.

The SEC claims that the whistleblower program has been a tremendous success by rooting out wrongdoing that it might not otherwise have uncovered. However, like any well-intentioned piece of legislation, the whistleblower law's unintended consequences may ultimately exceed its benefits.

A. <u>Whistleblower Awards.</u> The SEC has awarded over $300 Million to informants who have provided information that has led to SEC sanctions. The Office of the Whistleblower continues to define the contours of who can claim whistleblower status, which has included corporate officers and CCOs.

SEC Seeks Expansion of Whistleblower Program (7/2/18)

The SEC has proposed expanding whistleblower awards to include deferred and non-prosecution agreements with the Department of Justice or a state attorney general in a criminal case as well as SEC settlements outside of a judicial or administrative proceeding. According to the SEC, the proposal would "ensure that whistleblowers are not disadvantaged because of the particular form of action" taken. The SEC also proposed allowing discretionary awards in smaller cases that would not otherwise qualify. The SEC whistleblower program, established by the Dodd-Frank Act, has ordered over $266 Million in 55 whistleblowers, although 40% has been paid out to only 3 awards.

We would prefer to see the SEC limit the snitch program, rather than expand it. While the logic behind the program makes sense, the SEC should also examine its unintended consequences including the disincentives to include all necessary employees in problem resolution and the growth of extortionist lawyers representing disgruntled employees.

Corporate Officer Awarded $475,000-$575,000 for Whistleblower Claim (3/3/15)

The SEC announced a whistleblower award of between $475,000 and $575,000 to a company officer that reported securities fraud information that resulted in an enforcement action. The officer only became eligible to receive a whistleblower award because the company failed to address the issue for more than 120 days after compliance personnel received the information. Andrew Ceresney, Director of the SEC's Division of Enforcement said, "Corporate officers have front row seats overseeing the activities of their companies, and this particular officer should be commended for stepping up to report a securities law violation when it became apparent that the company's internal compliance system was not functioning well enough to address it."

This type of case should help internal compliance staff because companies that don't take the internal process seriously could face an SEC enforcement action arising from an officer's whistleblower claim.

Compliance Officer Receives $1.4-$1.6 Million Whistleblower Award (4/23/15)

The SEC awarded $1.4-$1.6 Million to a compliance officer that acted as a whistleblower against the whistleblower's company. According to the SEC, the compliance officer reported misconduct "after responsible management…became aware of potentially impending harm to investors and failed to take steps to prevent it." According to the SEC, this is the second award to an internal audit or compliance professional.

Allowing compliance officers to receive whistleblower awards changes their role in the regulatory system. Knowing that compliance officers have this regulatory club, management may begin to treat compliance officers as adverse parties. This is yet another reason why firms should consider the third-party compliance model, where an outside and independent firm audits a firm's regulatory compliance.

Report Suggests Whistleblower Statutes Affect Behavior Even Without Awards (6/11/14)

The law firm Davis Polk has published whistleblower data showing the limited success whistleblowers have in collecting awards. Davis Polk, in its paper titled "Recent Developments in Whistleblower Protections: Legal Analysis and Practical Implications," reports that only 20 of the 1846 Sarbanes-Oxley whistleblower actions filed with the Department of Labor since 2005 have been completed with a finding of "merit" and approximately 100 are listed as "settled." Regardless, Davis Polk argues that the whistleblower protections under Sarbanes-Oxley, Dodd-Frank, and the CFPA, have a behavioral effect on regulated entities (and their vendors) because of reputational risk as well as the fear that the SEC will use whistleblower claims as leverage in regulatory proceedings: "We would accordingly expect perceived retaliatory conduct to significantly affect the risk and settlement value of regulatory investigations, raising the stakes far beyond the statutorily defined civil remedies." Davis Polk also argues that the whistleblower statutes have a chilling effect on employers when dealing with problem employees.

Compliance officers should implement some of the practical advice that Davis Polk offers to address whistleblower claims. These include strong internal investigation and reporting mechanisms, employee hotlines, and consistent HR review policies.

❑ The List: Ten Important Facts about the SEC Whistleblower Program

Ten Important Facts about the SEC Whistleblower Program

1.	The SEC has awarded more than $326 Million to 59 whistleblowers.
2.	The largest whistleblower award to date is $83 Million.
3.	A whistleblower is entitled to 10-30 percent of monetary sanctions if the sanctions imposed exceed $1 Million.
4.	Both an outsider and a former employee can be a whistleblower.
5.	Covered firms may not take retaliatory job action against a whistleblower.
6.	Employee separation and noncompete agreements may not limit an employee's whistleblower rights.

7.	Directors can be liable for whistleblower retaliation.
8.	Internal reporting is not sufficient to become a protected whistleblower.
9.	In-house counsel and compliance officers are entitled to whistleblower protections.
10.	Firms must adopt whistleblower procedures.

B. <u>Retaliation</u>. Companies cannot take any retaliatory job action against a whistleblower. However, the Supreme Court has ruled that an informant must go to the SEC, and not just report internally, to benefit from whistleblower protections.

Supreme Court Rules that Whistleblower Must Report to SEC (*Digital Realty Trust v. Somers*; 2/22/18)

The United States Supreme Court has ruled that Dodd-Frank's anti-retaliation provisions apply only to whistleblowers who report the misconduct to the SEC. In the case, the employee brought a claim under Dodd-Frank's whistleblower anti-retaliation provisions, even though he had not reported to the SEC, because he claimed that he was fired as a result of reporting to management suspected securities law violations. The Supreme Court reversed the decision of the Ninth Circuit based on the plain reading of the statute which defines "whistleblower" as any individual who provides information relating to a violation of the securities laws to the SEC. The Court rejected the SEC rule that expanded anti-retaliation protection to those who only report internally. Looking at legislative history, the Court reasoned that "Dodd-Frank's award program and anti-retaliation provision thus work synchronously to motivate individuals with knowledge of illegal activity" to report to the SEC.

We restate our opinion that the Court is correct on the law even though Congress probably did want to protect those who only reported internally. Regardless, companies should still avoid retaliating against internal whistleblowers because (i) good companies should want to ferret out wrongdoing by encouraging employees to come forward and (ii) other laws and rules (e.g. state employment laws, Sarbanes-Oxley) could serve as the basis for a lawsuit.

General Counsel Awarded $7.9 Million for Wrongful Whistleblower Termination (*Wadler v. Bio-Rad*; 2/13/17)

A jury awarded a terminated General Counsel $2.9 Million in compensatory damages and $5 Million in punitive damages for wrongful termination due to his whistleblower activities. In a key ruling, the Court (USDC for Northern District of California) ruled not to exclude evidence provided by the GC that his former employer claimed was privileged under California professional rules. The Court held that federal law preempted the more stringent state law and that federal common law governing privilege applied to his Sarbanes-Oxley Act whistleblower retaliation claim. The GC had raised Foreign Corrupt Practices Act compliance concerns.

While we sympathize with the plaintiff in this case, the broader policy of piercing lawyer-client privilege may result in limiting the role of in-house counsel. Because the court can discard privilege, senior management and outside counsel may be less likely to include in-house lawyers in more sensitive matters.

Company Fined for Whistleblower Retaliation (*In re International Game Technology*; 10/11/16)

The SEC fined a public company $500,000 for terminating and otherwise retaliating against a whistleblower who claimed financial statements may have been misstated. The whistleblower reported his concerns to management, an internal hotline and, ultimately, to the SEC. The company limited certain career opportunities and finally terminated him after an internal investigation found that the company's financial statements were not misstated. The employee had received consistently positive performance reviews. The SEC claims that the job actions violated the whistleblower anti-retaliation provisions of the Dodd-Frank Act.

Dodd-Frank protects whistleblowers even if their assertions are later determined to be incorrect. Notably, the respondent agreed to pay a fine to the SEC. What about the aggrieved whistleblower? We assume he will hire a lawyer and file a claim for wrongful discharge, if he hasn't already sued or settled.

Federal Court Rules that Directors Can Be Liable for Whistleblower Retaliation (*Wadler v. Bio-Rad;* 10/29/15)

The United States District Court for the Northern District of California has ruled that a corporate whistleblower can bring an anti-retaliation claim against individual Directors under Sarbanes-Oxley and Dodd-Frank. The Court, acknowledging statutory ambiguity, drew on legislative intent to conclude that Directors should not be excluded from the definition of "employer" under the statutes because, otherwise, a company could avoid the anti-retaliation provisions simply by acting through its Board. In the case under review, the General Counsel claimed that the Board fired him as retaliation for pursuing concerns about violations of the Foreign Corrupt Practices Act.

Expect challenges to this decision and principle both in the Ninth Circuit and elsewhere as Directors (and their insurers) will want to avoid liability. Most interesting is whether the SEC will jump into this fight on either side i.e. looking to protect the independent directors or whistleblowers. As a practice point, firms must understand that whistleblowers must be treated like any other protected class, and courts will heavily scrutinize any job action following whistleblowing activity.

SEC Brings First Case for Retaliating Against Dodd-Frank Whistleblower (*In re Paradigm Capital Management;* 6/17/14)

A hedge fund manager was fined and ordered to pay restitution aggregating over $2 Million and hire an independent consultant for taking retaliatory job actions against a whistleblower related to trading conflicts of interest. The SEC charges that the respondent forced the firm's head trader to resign after discovering that he reported securities laws violations to the SEC. The head trader/whistleblower notified the SEC that the firm engaged in principal transactions with a proprietary account at a broker-dealer controlled by the respondent's principal. The SEC asserts that the firm did not obtain sufficient consent from the hedge fund by submitting it for approval by the general partner's conflicts committee staffed by personnel reporting to firm management. Apparently on the advice of the firm's employment counsel, the firm removed the whistleblower from his position as head trader, took away his email account, barred him from the premises, and then demoted him into a make-work assistant compliance position from which he ultimately resigned. The Dodd-Frank Act prohibits retaliation against employees acting as whistleblowers.

Dodd-Frank's whistleblower provisions should make firms consider implementing an element of independence into their compliance programs. Whether a firm hires an independent third-party compliance provider or ensures that the CCO reports to an independent board, registrants need to give potential whistleblowers an outlet to uncover regulatory issues without being forced to go straight to the regulator. Separately, private fund sponsors should note that GP approval of principal transactions will not cure the conflict of interest.

C. <u>Employee Restrictions</u>. Firms may not force employees to sign agreements that in any way limit their future rights to report wrongdoing to the SEC.

SEC Imposes $1.4 Million Fine for Whistleblower Rule Violations (*In re SandRidge Energy*; 12/21/16)

The SEC fined a public company $1.4 Million because its severance agreements violated the Dodd-Frank's whistleblower rules and because it retaliated against an internal whistleblower. The SEC maintains that the firm's severance agreements, which included non-disparagement and confidentiality provisions, violated the whistleblower rules because they impeded severed employees from communicating with the SEC. Also, the SEC asserts that the respondent terminated an internal whistleblower for raising concerns about how the firm calculated oil and gas reserves. The SEC's Whistleblower Chief noted, "This is the first time a company is being charged for retaliating against an internal whistleblower."

In addition to the retaliation action, the SEC, for the first time this year, imposes a 7+ figure fine for violating the whistleblower rules. As we predicted (see http://cipperman.com/2016/12/02/friday-list-2017-predictions/), the SEC continues to bring more cases assessing punitive fines for violations of the whistleblower rules. Compliance officers should review severance agreements and internal complaint processes.

SEC Risk Alert Warns About Whistleblower Policies and Practices (10/26/16)

The SEC's Office of Compliance Inspections and Examinations has issued a Risk Alert notifying advisers and broker-dealers that examination staff will examine whether agreements and other documents limit whistleblowers in violation of the Dodd-Frank Act. The staff will examine compliance manuals, codes of ethics, and employment and severance agreements to determine whether any provisions directly or indirectly impede an employee or former employee from communicating potential securities laws violations to the SEC. For example, the staff will assess whether confidentiality agreements include exceptions for SEC reporting or provisions requiring an employee to represent that s/he has not assisted with an investigation. The Risk Alert recommends immediate remedial measures including revising documents and notifying both current and former employees about their unrestricted right to report to the SEC. The SEC has brought several cases during the last year alleging that a registrant's practices violated Dodd-Frank's whistleblower provisions.

Our most recent C-suite survey reported that 91% of respondents have not changed their compliance programs due to whistleblower concerns. (See http://cipperman.com/wp-content/uploads/2016C-SuiteSurveyResuts.pdf). Compli-pros should add policies and procedures that ensure that whistleblowers are in no way impeded by company documents. Then, firms should test the policies by reviewing agreements and interviewing current and former employees.

Large Asset Manager Pays $340,000 Fine because Separation Agreements Violated Whistleblower Rule (*In re Blackrock*; 1/19/17)

The SEC fined a large asset manager $340,000 because it added provisions to its separation agreements prohibiting employees who received severance payments from collecting whistleblower awards. The SEC contends that the respondent added the provisions after the SEC adopted the Dodd-Frank rule prohibiting any action that could impede a potential whistleblower. The SEC imposed the fine even though the respondent voluntarily changed the language and even without any evidence that any employee was actually impeded or that the respondent ever sought to enforce the restrictions. An SEC official faulted the firm for taking "direct aim at our whistleblower program by using separation agreements that removed the financial incentives for reporting problems to the SEC."

Registrants must immediately review and revise confidentiality and separation agreements to strike any potentially violative language.

D. Third-Party Whistleblowers. A whistleblower can be a former employee or a third party. A cottage industry has emerged for contingency-fee securities litigators that encourage whistleblowers to file claims.

SEC Awards $700,000 Whistleblower Award to Company Outsider (1/26/16)

The SEC approved a $700,000 whistleblower award to a company outsider that "conducted a detailed analysis that led to a successful SEC enforcement action." The SEC's Enforcement Director, Andrew Ceresney, explained, "The voluntary submission of high quality analysis by industry experts can be every bit as valuable as firsthand knowledge of wrongdoing by company insiders." Sean X. McKessy, Chief of the SEC's Office of the Whistleblower, said that the SEC welcomes "analytical information from those with in depth market knowledge and experience that may provide the springboard for an investigation."

Now registrants must worry about outsiders reviewing their actions and using the SEC's whistleblower framework to collect big awards. Although we don't think Congress intended this type of back-door private right of action, the SEC apparently welcomes third-party information and claims.

Former Employee Receives Reduced Whistleblower Award (11/5/15)

The SEC awarded $325,000 to an investment firm whistleblower even though the whistleblower did not report the violations until after leaving employment. The SEC indicated that it reduced the award percentage because it found the delay unreasonable but still granted the award because it led to a successful enforcement action. The SEC explained, "We did not decrease Claimant's award percentage because [redacted] declined to report internally, but because after becoming aware of the wrongdoing, [redacted] did nothing to report the information and did nothing to try to stop the violations from continuing to occur, which under the facts and circumstances, we find unreasonable."

This is a controversial decision for both registrants and whistleblowers. Registrants now must fear that a disgruntled former employee could seek revenge through a bogus whistleblower claim without ever having raised an issue during the time of employment. Yet, legitimate whistleblowers get penalized if they want to avoid a current employer's wrath by waiting until leaving before reporting.

SEC Official Encourages Competitive Whistleblowing and Their Lawyers (9/15/16)

The SEC's Enforcement Director, Andrew Ceresney, lauded the SEC's whistleblower program while encouraging competitive whistleblowing and lawyers that represent whistleblowers. Mr. Ceresney expressed his appreciation for whistleblowers, the success of the program, and its "transformative impact." Although approximately half of award recipients were current or former employees of companies for which they reported wrongdoing, Mr. Ceresney also encouraged whistleblowing by company outsiders who have in-depth market knowledge. Mr. Ceresney also lauded whistleblower lawyers who help manage client expectations and ensure confidentiality.

Mr. Ceresney's comments may hasten the spread of competitive whistleblowing whereby industry competitors use the SEC's enforcement mechanics to hobble a rival. Also, encouraging whistleblowing lawyers could revive the same sort of securities class action lawyers that plagued the securities markets in the 1980s and 1990s.

FIVE ACTION ITEMS:

1. Create internal procedures for up-the-chain reporting and claims handling similar to the procedures used for Sarbanes-Oxley.

2. Move quickly to acknowledge claims and address them. Delays may frustrate the potential whistleblower and make your firm look indifferent to regulatory issues.

3. Review offer letters and severance agreements, and include language that specifically allows current and former employees to provide information to the SEC.

4. When discussing sensitive issues, limit access to those who have a need to know and avoid careless emails. Consider including outside counsel.

5. Once it is clear that a whistleblower has reported to the SEC, retain a lawyer that specializes in employment law and understands the legal definition of "retaliation."

TREND

10

FINRA has emerged as an enforcement power.

Before the rapid expansion of mutual funds and fee-based advisers, FINRA (formerly known as NASD) served as the primary regulator of those providing investment advice to retail investors. Since 1939, NASD/FINRA has supervised broker-dealers in areas including sales practices, suitability, and supervision. In 2007, FINRA, formed from the consolidation of NASD and NYSE enforcement, morphed from a quasi-private membership organization into a securities enforcement regulator. Today, it competes with the SEC for securities enforcement hegemony, even though the SEC technically regulates FINRA.

To ensure its continuity, FINRA relies on fees and fines rather than the taxpayer money that funds the SEC. As a consequence, FINRA has a financial incentive to impose fines to support its operations. In the fiscal year ending in mid-2017, FINRA assessed over $170 Million in fines as compared to about $93 Million the prior year—an 82 percent increase. FINRA reported that the increase in fines and restitution (another $28 Million) helped fill a growing funding gap caused by shrinking operating revenues from fees collected.

> **FINRA reported that the increase in fines and restitution … helped fill a growing funding gap caused by shrinking operating revenues from fees collected.**

Fed up with the increasing actions and fines, many industry participants have begun to colloquially refer to the regulator as "FINE-RA."

Industry griping has led to Congressional scrutiny. During oversight hearings, both Democrats and Republicans have questioned FINRA's operations and enforcement activities. They have also asked whether enforcement proceeds should go back to harmed investors rather than toward FINRA's operations. Several Congressmen also questioned the large salaries paid to FINRA leaders as well as FINRA's status as a nongovernmental entity.

FINRA has done little to dispel industry concerns. Every year, FINRA publishes an ever-expanding list of examination priorities. Industry executives and compli-pros must often interpret a growing list of requirements that could result in firm or career-ending enforcement cases.

Over the last several years, FINRA has rivaled SEC Enforcement for harsh fines and penalties. FINRA has imposed multimillion-dollar fines and restitution orders alleging a wide variety of wrongdoing.

FINRA has followed the SEC in assessing multimillion-dollar penalties against brokerage firms charged with recommending higher-fee mutual fund share classes when less expensive share classes were available. FINRA fined Merrill Lynch $8 Million (in addition to forcing $89 Million in refunds) for failing to provide sales charge waivers and offer the lowest share class to certain qualified accounts. FINRA has launched similar cases against Barclay's, Wells Fargo, Raymond James, and LPL, which together have agreed to pay $43.75 Million in fines and restitution.

FINRA has always prosecuted failure-to-supervise cases, but in recent years has imposed much heftier fines. In *UBS Financial Services*, FINRA assessed $35 Million in penalties because the firm failed to stop a broker from encouraging clients to borrow from an affiliated bank to purchase closed-end funds. Other big fines included $5 Million for IPO sales violations (*In re Morgan Stanley Smith Barney*), $3.75 Million for hiring a bad broker and ignoring red flags about him (*In re Oppenheimer*), $15 Million for allowing research analysts to misuse information (*In re Citigroup Global Markets*), and $11.7 Million for failing to monitor product sales (*In re LPL Financial*).

FINRA has also used suitability—another common allegation—to collect fines that far exceed what FINRA would assess in the old days before the merger. In *MetLife Securities*, FINRA assessed $25 Million in fines and restitution related to variable annuity switching transactions. In *Santander Securities*, the firm agreed to pay $6.3 Million when FINRA accused it of failing to reduce client holdings of certain bonds. In *Oppenheimer*, FINRA imposed $2.9 Million in penalties based on allegations that the broker-dealer failed to follow its own policies about the sales of complex ETFs.

Other areas of FINRA regulation—best execution, anti-money laundering, reporting, net capital, and operations—have led to eye-popping fines. FINRA imposed a $2.5 Million penalty on Citigroup for failed best execution testing and a $17 Million fine on Raymond James for failing to devote adequate resources to AML monitoring. Macquarie agreed to pay nearly $3 Million for inaccurate blue sheet reporting, Charles Schwab paid $2 Million for miscalculated net capital, and Deutsche Bank agreed to a $6 Million fine for providing inaccurate trade data to the regulator as a result of programming errors.

We don't expect this trend to abate soon. During the debate about the DOL fiduciary rule, FINRA volunteered itself as the regulator of choice to enforce a uniform fiduciary standard. Over the last several years, FINRA has expanded the suitability standard beyond a point-of-sale analysis to an ongoing obligation that has taken on fiduciary overtones. As the SEC seeks to increase the number of advisory exams, FINRA has advocated for an expanded mandate to regulate, supervise, and examine advisers. Bottom line? Regulators like to regulate.

A. <u>Fines and Priorities</u>. FINRA has assessed record penalties, which have been used to offset declining operating revenues. Also, FINRA's examination and enforcement priorities keep expanding.

FINRA Imposed $80 Million More in Fines in 2016 (7/6/17)

FINRA imposed nearly double the fines on the industry in 2016, assessing $173.8 Million in fines as compared to $93.8 Million in 2015, according to its annual report. The increase in fines helped FINRA report over $57 Million in net income versus a $39 Million loss last year, even though operating income was lower in 2016. FINRA also ordered another $27.9 Million in restitution. FINRA uses fines collected for "capital expenditures and regulatory projects."

Most of the financial regulators use their enforcement powers to collect funds to support their activities. Rather than encourage this financial incentive to bring cases, policy-makers should consider other alternatives such as third-party compliance reviews or user fees.

FINRA Issues Examinations Findings Report (12/7/17)

FINRA has issued a report summarizing its observations on the compliance and supervision issues arising from recent examinations. Highlighted concerns include cybersecurity, outside business activities, anti-money laundering, product suitability, best execution, and alternatives in IRA accounts. FINRA found weaknesses in cybersecurity programs including failure to control access to data, insufficient risk assessments, and inadequate vendor supervision. FINRA expressed concerns about failures to report OBAs and failures to execute adequate reviews or retain documentation. AML programs fell behind as firms changed and grew but failed to properly resource growing AML volume. FINRA raised suitability concerns over recommendations of UITs, fund share classes, and complex products. FINRA hopes that firms will use the report as a "resource in tailoring their compliance and supervisory programs to their business."

It's always good to get more transparency into the examination program. What's less clear is how firms should react to this information especially since FINRA generally issues its examination priorities letter in January.[28] Regardless, expect FINRA to focus on these issues during cycle exams.

FINRA Releases Annual Exam Priorities Letter (1/9/18)

FINRA released its annual Regulatory and Examination Priorities Letter identifying areas of FINRA focus for 2018. FINRA announced a focus on fraud including insider trading, microcap pump-and-dump, Ponzi schemes and the resulting referrals to the SEC, even if the wrongdoing is outside of FINRA's jurisdiction. FINRA will also target supervision practices including the hiring and review of high-risk brokers, branch offices, and outside business activities. New this year is a focus on cryptocurrency offerings and the role registered reps play in effecting transactions. FINRA also highlights best execution, cybersecurity, anti-money laundering, and business continuity. Consistent with prior years, FINRA will devote resources to customer protection and net capital, suitability, and liquidity risk.

Compli-pros should use the Priorities Letter as a checklist to review the Written Supervisory Procedures. FINRA generally means what it says and addresses these topics during exams.

B. <u>Harsh Penalties</u>. FINRA has imposed large penalties in areas that used to be technical violations resulting in deficiencies or censures.

1. *Mutual fund share classes*

BD to Pay Over $97 Million for Mutual Fund Share Class Violations (*In re Merrill Lynch*; 6/18/14)

A large broker-dealer agreed to refund $89 Million to investors and pay an additional $8 Million fine for failing to waive sales charges and failing

---

28   FINRA released its exam priorities a month later, but FINRA did not reconcile the issues raised with its priorities.

to offer the lowest mutual fund share class available. According to FINRA, the firm's failures affected 41,000 small business retirement plan accounts and 6,800 charities. FINRA alleges that the firm knew about the overcharging as early as 2006 but failed to adopt and implement policies and procedures to ensure the financial advisers waived the sales charges or offered lower cost share classes. Brad Bennett, FINRA's Executive Vice President and Chief of Enforcement, said that "investors must be able to trust that their brokerage firm will offer the lowest-cost share classes available to them."

The SEC and FINRA have recently stepped up their warnings that brokers and wrap sponsors must offer the least expensive mutual fund share class for each investor. Compliance should ensure that the firm has adopted and implemented effective policies and procedures that will withstand regulatory scrutiny.

BD Will Pay $13.75 Million for Unsuitable Mutual Fund Recommendations (*In re Barclay's*; 12/30/15)

A large broker-dealer agreed to pay $13.75 Million in disgorgement, fines, and interest for unsuitable mutual fund recommendations and allowing improper fund switching. FINRA alleges that the firm improperly defined the term "mutual fund switch," thereby allowing over 6,000 unsuitable switching transactions over a 5-year period. FINRA also alleges that the firm failed its suitability obligations in nearly 40% of recommendations and often failed to provide mutual fund breakpoint discounts.

We recommend that firms conduct an annual, independent review of suitability compliance in order to uncover systemic failures.

FINRA Orders 3 Firms to Pay $30 Million for Not Waiving Mutual Fund Sales Loads (*In re Wells Fargo, Raymond James, and LPL*; 7/7/15)

FINRA ordered three large broker-dealers to pay a combined $30 million in restitution to retirement and charitable accounts entitled to mutual fund sales load waivers. Over 50,000 accounts purchased lower-fee Class A shares since 2009 but did not receive the waivers described in the prospectuses. According to FINRA, the firms "unreasonably relied on financial advisors to waive charges for retirement and eligible charitable organization accounts, without providing them with critical information and training."

Firms cannot issue compliance edicts and rely on sales personnel to execute them. Firms must train the affected personnel, create systems that prevent violations, and test compliance on a regular basis. Otherwise, firms will get tagged for failing to supervise.

2. Failure to supervise

Large BD to Pay $35 Million for Failing to Supervise (*In re UBS Financial Services*; 10/7/15)

A large broker-dealer agreed to pay nearly $35 Million to settle SEC and FINRA charges that it failed to supervise a broker that encouraged customers to borrow from an affiliated bank to purchase proprietary closed-end funds. Although the broker received compensation when his clients secured the loans, customers were prohibited from using loan proceeds to purchase securities. The SEC alleges that the broker encouraged customers to bypass this restriction by routing the loan funds through a third-party bank, thereby escaping detection. The scheme ultimately came to light when the closed-end funds declined in value and customers complained about margin calls. The SEC alleges that the respondent ignored red flags including outsized loan production in the offending office.

Perhaps the bigger mistake was compensating brokers for encouraging customers to secure loans from an affiliated bank. The respondent practically encouraged its brokers to violate its own policies.

Firm to Pay $3.75 Million for Negligent Broker Due Diligence and Supervision (*In re Oppenheimer*; 3/30/15)

A large broker-dealer agreed to pay a $2.5 Million fine and an additional $1.25 Million in restitution for failing to supervise a broker and timely filing U4s and U5s. FINRA charges the broker with failing to properly investigate the broker before hiring him, relying solely on the CRD system rather than conducting a criminal background check and surveying court records, which would have uncovered significant reportable events. The broker ultimately stole money from clients, which, according to FINRA, could have been stopped had the firm adequately followed up on red flags such as excessive trading and unauthorized wire transfers. Separately, FINRA also alleges the firm had a systemic breakdown with respect to filing U4s and U5s, thereby misleading the public about hundreds of allegation against its brokers. The firm's legal department failed to timely file the U4s and U5s even though it had knowledge of its failings.

Firms need to retain compliance professionals responsible for conducting rep due diligence and making the necessary filings. Otherwise, these seemingly mundane tasks, when done improperly, could endanger your firm.

Investment Bank Will Pay $15 Million for Failing to Enforce Discipline against Research Analysts (*In re Citigroup Global Markets*; 12/2/14)

A large investment bank agreed to pay $15 Million for failing to enforce its procedures prohibiting research analysts from selectively providing information to clients. According to FINRA, the firm allowed research analysts to attend "idea dinners" where they shared stock tips and related information with clients. In many cases, the information and recommendations were inconsistent with published research reports. The firm did have policies and procedures prohibiting the dissemination of this type of material nonpublic information, but, according to FINRA, the firm failed to adequately implement the procedures by failing to impose discipline after several warnings or long after the conduct occurred. Consequently, violators tended to ignore the warnings and continue to engage in the unlawful conduct.

Firms need to take immediate disciplinary action against individuals that violate firm policies and procedures. This could include memos in the personnel file, bonus reductions, fines, suspension, and termination. Otherwise regulators will fault the firm for a lax internal control environment.

Firm Pays $11.7 Million and Hires More than 200 Compli-Pros to Settle Charges (*In re LPL Financial*; 5/8/15)

A large broker-dealer has agreed to pay at least $11.7 Million in fines and restitution and has hired over 200 compliance and risk management personnel to settle a broad range of failure to supervise allegations. FINRA charges the firm with failing to (i) supervise and monitor sales of complex products including ETFs, (ii) deliver millions of trade confirmations, (iii) detect suspicious AML activities, (iv) review advertising and communications, and (v) monitor customer accounts for holding periods and concentrations. Brad Bennett, FINRA Executive Vice President and Chief of Enforcement, said, "LPL's supervisory breakdowns resulted from a sustained failure to devote sufficient resources to compliance programs." As part of the remediation, the firm has hired over 200 compliance and risk professionals in the last two years, a 53% increase in staff. It has also agreed to pay a $10 Million fine and $1.7 in restitution, which could increase as FINRA continues its review of ETF sales practices.

Firms should note the focus on supervisory and compliance infrastructure rather than on specific customer harm. The regulators will come down hard on firms that don't build an adequate compliance department.

3. Best execution

BD Failed to Conduct Best Execution Testing of Flawed Execution System (*In re Citigroup Global Markets*; 9/4/14)

A large broker-dealer agreed to pay approximately $2.5 Million in penalties, restitution, and interest for failing to conduct best execution reviews. According to FINRA, the respondent's order execution system utilized a faulty pricing logic that failed to include the National Best Bid and Offer for non-convertible preferred securities. FINRA alleges that the firm knew about its best execution issues but did not perform best execution reviews. FINRA also charges the firm with compliance failures because its Written Supervisory Procedures did not specifically identify the person responsible for best execution reviews, how reviews were to be undertaken, and how such reviews should be documented.

Firms must create a dynamic nexus between Compliance and IT. Compliance personnel must understand the technology that underlies operational systems, and IT personnel must understand the rules and regulations as they design and implement systems. Otherwise, breakdowns like this occur and nobody knows how it happened or who is responsible.

Online Broker Fined $900,000 for Poor Best Execution Testing (*In re E*Trade Securities*; 6/8/16)

A large online broker was fined $900,000 for failing to conduct adequate best execution reviews of its order routing. FINRA faults the firm for failing to consider order flow sent to an affiliated execution broker as well as the affiliate's ability to redirect order flow. Although the firm's best execution committee compared its execution quality "with certain industry and custom averages," it did not focus on "comparisons to the actual execution quality provided by the market centers" to which it routed trades. Thomas Gira, FINRA's Head of Market Regulation, said that a best execution review needs to be "a substance over form review, not a form over substance review."

When firms route orders to affiliates, they must increase best execution testing and review to ensure that the regulator cannot second-guess a process that appears to have an embedded conflict of interest.

4. Anti-money laundering

BD Fined $17 Million and Compliance Officer Fined and Suspended for AML Monitoring Weaknesses (*In re Raymond James*; 5/19/16)

A large broker-dealer was fined $17 Million and its AML Compliance Officer was fined and suspended for widespread failures in the firm's anti-money laundering compliance program. FINRA faults the firm for failing to devote adequate resources to AML compliance as the firm grew rapidly from 2002-2013. According to FINRA, the respondent relied on a few employees to manually review millions of transactions. Also, the AML Compliance Officer relied on an affiliate's AML efforts without adequate testing and assurances of compliance. FINRA also noted that the firm was cited and fined in 2012 for AML compliance breakdowns that it undertook, but failed, to correct. FINRA charges failure to implement an adequate AML program and supervisory structure including reasonable policies and procedures.

Compliance is not a "set it and forget it" function. As firms grow and change, they must add resources to ensure they continue to implement best practices. We recommend that firms re-examine allocations at least annually and devote no less than 5% of revenue to compliance.

Large BD/Custodian Fined $8 Million and AML CCO Fined and Suspended over AML Compliance Issues (*In re Brown Brothers Harriman*; 2/13/14)

FINRA fined a large broker-dealer/custodian $8 Million and fined and suspended its AML Compliance Officer for several anti-money laundering compliance failures related to penny stock transactions. FINRA alleges that the firm allowed foreign banks in tax havens to establish undisclosed omnibus account through which questionable underlying customers could manipulate penny stocks. FINRA criticizes the firm and the AML CCO for an AML compliance program that failed to uncover or report suspicious trading even though the firm had an AML compliance staff and used several technology and testing tools. FINRA cites internal compliance memos indicating that the AML compliance staff knew of the risks and recommend the firm stop the trading, which the firm ultimately did in 2013.

This action is about as frightening as it gets for CCOs. According to FINRA, the AML CCO knew about the risky trading, advised management to stop, and implemented compliance procedures to test for suspicious activities. FINRA's fundamental charge is that the compliance program could not have been adequate because it missed the illegal trading. The net result is that the AML CCO is strictly liable for AML failures. This type of case suggests that CCOs must become the hall monitors or firm police officers rather than regulatory advisers responsible for implementing policies and procedures.

FINRA Fines BD $550,000 for Weak AML Procedures Related to DVP Accounts (*In re Aegis Capital*; 4/24/18)

FINRA fined a broker-dealer $550,000 for failing to properly monitor and detect red flags related to small cap securities traded via delivery versus payment accounts. According to FINRA, the respondent did not implement the same level of due diligence as it utilized with accounts held at the broker-dealer. FINRA also alleges that the firm failed to enhance its compliance procedures even after warnings from the SEC and its clearing firm. FINRA faults the firm for over-relying on branch managers to conduct surveillance and report red flags.

It's never a good idea to rely on producers or their supervisors to monitor activities. They are not regulatory professionals, and they often have a significant conflict of interest with respect to activities that affect their compensation.

5. Reporting

Firm Fined $2.95 Million for Mis-Reporting Trade Data to FINRA (*In re Macquarie Capital*; 12/29/15)

FINRA fined a broker-dealer affiliate of a global asset management firm $2.95 Million for failing to provide accurate "blue sheet" trading data when requested over a 3-year period. FINRA alleges that the firm experienced "multiple problems" with its electronic systems, resulting mis-reporting of buys and sells, miscalculating net amounts, and failing to provide accurate customer information. FINRA also faults the firm for failing to implement an adequate audit system. FINRA Executive Vice President and Head of FINRA's Office of Fraud Detection and Market Intelligence, Cameron Funkhouser, advised, "All introducing and clearing firms should take inventory of their processes for producing accurate trading data to ensure that they are in position to comply with blue sheet requests from regulators in a complete and timely manner."

The regulators will impose significant fines for even technical violations where they feel the firm has failed to take stock of internal controls, especially over long periods of time.

BD Pays $3.4 Million to Settle Charges Including Failing to File Regulatory Info (*In re Oppenheimer*; 11/30/16)

A large broker-dealer agreed to pay $3.4 Million to settle charges that included failure to report over 350 significant regulatory events to FINRA in a timely manner. FINRA alleges that over an 8-year period, the respondent failed to timely report securities law violations, employee disciplinary actions, and securities litigation settlements. FINRA also faults the firm for failing to file copies of civil complaints and arbitration claims. The firm also failed to notify FINRA that its AML compliance officer and another employee received Wells notices. FINRA rules require the filing of such information within 30 days. FINRA's Enforcement Chief explained, "FINRA uses this information to identify and initiate investigations of firms and associated persons that pose a risk to investors."

Back in the bad old days, failing to file information may have prompted an unpleasant phone call or, perhaps, a nasty letter. Now, such failings can result in multi-million-dollar fines.

6. Suitability

Insurance BD to Pay $25 Million to Settle VA Sales Misreps (*In re MetLife Securities*; 5/6/16)

A large insurance-affiliated broker-dealer agreed to pay $25 Million in fines and restitution in connection with variable annuity replacement transactions, which includes the largest fine ever imposed relating to variable annuities. FINRA asserts that, over a 5-year period, the respondent misrepresented material facts about expenses, features, and death benefits in 72% of replacement transactions. FINRA also avers that the firm's principals approved 99.79% of VA replacement applications even though nearly three quarters contained materially inaccurate information. FINRA also faults the firm for failing to adequately train its registered reps.

The regulators will shine a very bright light on sales of complex investment products that enrich the registered rep and the firm. The DoL has already promulgated its version of a fiduciary duty. Will the SEC and FINRA be far behind?

BD Will Pay $6.3 Million for Failing to Monitor Client Concentrations Following Market Events (*In re Santander Securities*; 10/16/15)

A large broker-dealer agreed to pay $6.3 Million in fines and disgorgement for failing to implement supervisory policies and procedures that would assess suitability after significant market events. FINRA alleges the firm significantly reduced its inventory of certain Puerto Rican municipal securities following market events including credit downgrades. However, the firm failed to reduce customer inventories, including closed-end funds managed by the respondent, and failed to change the bonds' suitability risk classification. FINRA also charges the firm with failing to supervise employee trading of the bonds.

FINRA interprets suitability as an ongoing obligation to monitor customer positions. In this case, the firm compounded the issue by reducing its own inventory without addressing client positions. FINRA essentially applies a fiduciary standard to brokers where the firm cannot benefit to a greater extent than its clients.

BD Pays $2.9 Million for Unsuitable ETF Sales (*In re Oppenheimer & Co.*; 6/23/16)

A large broker-dealer agreed to pay over $2.9 Million in fines and disgorgement for failing to follow its policies and procedures regarding the sales of leveraged, inverse, and inverse-leveraged ETFs. The firm adopted relevant compliance policies and procedures regarding retail sales of non-traditional ETFs following a FINRA Regulatory Notice in 2009. However, FINRA asserts that since that time, more than 760 reps executed more than 30,000 non-traditional ETF transactions totaling $1.7 Billion. FINRA faults the firm for failing to train its reps, prevent the unlawful sales, conduct surveillance, or perform adequate reasonable basis suitability due diligence. Brad Bennett, FINRA Chief of Enforcement, said, "Written procedures are worthless unless accompanied by a program to enforce them."

A compliance program does not stop at well-drafted policies and procedures. That's the easy part. The real compliance work involves enforcing those policies through operations, training, testing, and reporting.

7. Net capital

Large Broker/Custodian Fined $2 Million for Overnight Net Capital Violations (*In re Charles Schwab & Co.*; 8/27/15)

FINRA fined a large broker/custodian $2 Million for violating its net capital requirements when it transferred overnight cash balances to its parent company. According to FINRA, the firm transferred $1 Billion for overnight investment and recorded the transaction as an unsecured loan. The transfer resulted in significant net capital deficiencies. According to FINRA, the firm's Treasury function failed to consult the Regulatory Reporting group. FINRA faults the firm for weak supervisory controls. Brad Bennett, FINRA's Executive Vice President and Chief of Enforcement, said, "Communication between risk functions within a firm is essential."

Lack of communication between separate functions affects many large firms. Without adequate executive oversight, firms can trip over regulatory wires.

Large BD Fined $3 Million for Faulty Reserve Calculations (*In re Pershing*; 1/5/15)

FINRA fined a large clearing firm $3 Million for miscalculating its reserve formula, resulting in reserve deficiencies ranging from $4 Million to $220 Million over an eight-month period. FINRA alleges that the firm included certain debit items even though they did not satisfy Rule 15c3-3's documentation requirements to include the items. FINRA also faults the firm's supervisory system and procedures for failing to implement a mechanism that reviewed procedural changes that led to the miscalculations.

This action follows several recent regulatory trends: (1) enforcement actions and large fines even though there is no customer or investor impact; (2) actions involving violations of highly technical and subjective regulatory requirements; (3) large fines for violations of net capital calculations and reserve requirements; and (4) faulting compliance systems for regulatory failures without an examination of whether such systems were reasonably designed.

8. *Operations*

Online Broker Fined $5.5 Million for Ignoring Short Sale Red Flags (*In re Interactive Brokers*; 8/22/18)

FINRA fined a global online broker $5.5 Million for allowing naked short selling in violation of Regulation SHO despite red flags raised by FINRA as well as its own compliance and internal audit departments. FINRA maintains that, over a three-year period, the BD did not timely close out fail-to-deliver positions, unlawfully routed short sale orders, and did not issue required client pre-borrow notices. The firm's Compliance Technology Department had advised senior management to fix systems that failed to account for segregation deficits. The firm's Internal Audit Department also highlighted deficiencies. FINRA noted red flags in three consecutive examinations.

The regulators will react swiftly and harshly to a registrant that knows about compliance problems but appears to flout the requirements by failing to take remedial action. When assessing compliance programs, senior executives should first ask whether the firm has addressed previously-identified deficiencies.

Weak Market Access Compliance Costs Broker-Dealer $1.5 Million (*In re Instinet*; 5/8/18)

A large broker-dealer agreed to pay $1.575 Million to FINRA and several exchanges for failing to implement procedures to properly control market access. FINRA asserts that the firm's weak procedures and controls allowed multiple instances of spoofing, wash trading, and access by unidentified traders. FINRA claims that the firm's Written Supervisory Procedures did not adequately describe how supervisors and others should follow up on red flags. FINRA charges the firm with violations of the customer protection rule (15c3-5) and the supervision/compliance rule (3110). FINRA explains that the market access rule is "designed to ensure that broker-dealers appropriately control the risks associated with market access, so as not to jeopardize their own financial condition, that of other market participants, the integrity of trading on the securities markets, and the stability of the financial system."

The market access rule is fairly specific about the supervisory and compliance requirements. Generalized WSPs and third-party technology half-measures won't satisfy the regulators or the exchanges. We call this "compliance alchemy": the appearance of a compliance infrastructure without actually stopping (or even facilitating) the targeted wrongdoing.

BD Fined $6.25 Million for Allowing Illegal Margin Lending (*In re Merrill Lynch*; 12/1/16)

FINRA fined a large broker-dealer $6.25 Million for failing to prevent customers from using lines of credit to purchase securities, thereby violating the margin rules. The BD offered a program whereby customers could borrow against their brokerage accounts and use the proceeds for purposes other than buying securities. However, FINRA alleges that the firm failed to implement adequate supervisory procedures to educate and train employees and customers and prevent the misuse of the lending proceeds. FINRA maintains that customers often borrowed and invested in securities within 14 days.

This case shows the difference between policies and procedures. A policy states a firm's position on a course of conduct or practice. Procedures are then required to implement that policy and ensure compliance. Firms that stop at broad policy statements have not implemented an adequate compliance program.

BD Smacked with $1.5 Million Fine for Failing to Properly Maintain Electronic Trading Records (*In re State Street Global Markets*; 9/19/17)

FINRA fined a large broker-dealer $1.5 Million for failing to properly maintain electronic brokerage records. According to FINRA, the respondent's ATS business failed to maintain over 100 million trading records in "write once, read only" (WORM) format over a 6-year period. FINRA also faults the BD for failing to maintain duplicate copies of over 300 million orders placed over the same period. The failures also resulted in charges that the firm did not have adequate audit or compliance procedures. FINRA said the required records and formats are necessary for regulatory examinations and internal audits.

The IT folks must connect with the compi-pros to understand the specific regulatory requirements for electronic data retention. Then, the compli-pros must determine how to implement effective audit and compliance surveillance. The most dangerous phrase in financial services: "That's not my job."

IT Failures Result in $6 Million Fine (*In re Deutsche Bank Securities*; 7/11/16)

FINRA fined a large investment bank $6 Million because programming errors resulted in the provision of inaccurate trade data to regulators over an 8-year period. FINRA asserts the firm misreported more than 1 million "blue sheet" transactions because of programming errors and failures to upgrade systems after regulatory changes. FINRA also faults the firm for failing to implement proper supervisory and audit systems. Regulators use the blue sheet data for regulatory and enforcement purposes including monitoring of insider trading.

One of the most-overlooked compliance risks involves the failure of IT systems to follow regulatory guidelines. A disconnect between the IT folks and the compli-pros can create serious systemic weakness.

Failed Manual Processes Result in $1 Million Fine for Large BD (*In re JP Morgan*; 4/21/16)

A large broker-dealer, together with its affiliate clearing firm, were fined $1,025,000 for several technical violations resulting from manual processes. FINRA charges the respondents with failing to (i) send investment objective change letters to customers, (ii) review outside brokerage accounts, (iii) send account opening letters, and (iv) send transaction confirmations. According to FINRA, the firm had relevant policies and procedures in place but failed to enforce those policies as a result of manual processes that allowed for human error.

This shows how operational holes can cause compliance violations. The firm had adequate policies but fallible humans that owned key steps in the process failed to fulfill their responsibilities.

❏ *The List: Ten Examples of Brokers Behaving Badly*

The debate about the now-vacated DoL fiduciary rule and the recently proposed Regulation Best Interest continues. We have argued that a uniform fiduciary standard should apply to both retail brokers and advisers. Why? We accept the position that retail consumers should not have to hire a lawyer to determine the advice standards to which his/her financial professional adheres. More significant, however, is that brokers behave badly and need a higher standard. An academic study that was first published in 2016 reported that 7% of broker-advisers have misconduct records, prior offenders are five times more likely to engage in misconduct, and 44 percent of brokers fired for misconduct are reemployed within a year.[29] The authors concluded: "We find that financial adviser misconduct is broader than a few heavily publicized scandals." They also argued that a more stringent standard would help the industry by improving the low reputation of financial professionals. Our reporting of cases also shows endemic broker misconduct. In the following list, we highlight examples of brokers behaving badly, which should inform the debate on a uniform fiduciary standard.

Ten Examples of Brokers Behaving Badly

1.	**Stealing from clients.** A broker exploited a weakness in his firm's control systems that allowed third-party disbursements, enabling him to misappropriate $7 Million from clients.[30]
2.	**Churning.** A broker recommended an unsuitable in-and-out trading strategy that generated significant commissions.
3.	**Misrepresenting disciplinary record:** A broker's website claimed he never had a complaint, even though several customers filed and settled complaints over the course of an 8-year period.
4.	**Misusing client information.** A broker shared nonpublic personal information (including holdings and cash balances) about clients with a person no longer affiliated with his firm.

---

29   *The Market for Financial Adviser Misconduct* (Egan, Matvos, and Seru (March 1, 2016)).

30   See blog for links to cases.

5.	**Revenue sharing.** A broker received undisclosed revenue sharing on mutual fund trades from the clearing broker.
6.	**Undisclosed markups/markdowns.** An interdealer failed to disclose markups and markdowns on securities traded for clients.
7.	**Commission kickbacks.** A trading supervisor demanded commission kickbacks from junior traders to whom he assigned clients.
8.	**Pump-and dump.** A broker engaged in an ongoing penny stock pump-and-dump scheme.
9.	**Bribing public officials.** A broker spent nearly $20,000 on hotels, meals and concert tickets to bribe a public plan official to secure brokerage business from the public plan.
10.	**IPO kickbacks.** A broker and his client conspired in a kickback scheme whereby the customer would pay back 24% of his profits in exchange for preferred IPO and secondary offering allocations.

FIVE ACTION ITEMS:

1. Draft, implement, and test detailed written supervisory procedures that specifically address FINRA priorities and FINRA's enforcement actions.

2. If your firm is dually registered, consider retaining two separate chief compliance officers, one of whom specializes in adviser regulation and the other specializing in broker-dealer regulation.

3. Review ongoing client relationships and interactions, and monitor broker conduct after the initial recommendation.

4. To satisfy your supervisory obligations, create an objective disciplinary system that holds reps accountable for bad behavior.

5. Develop a stand-alone anti-money laundering compliance program.

Predictions for 2019 and Beyond

As I said at the beginning of this book, any discussion of regulatory trends necessarily starts at a moment in time and looks backward. By the time you read this, the trends identified will have already changed and new ones will have emerged. My goal in writing this book was to give investment management professionals some perspective and insight on their current regulatory environment so that they could protect their businesses against regulatory risk.

Yet I have greater ambitions, too. The SEC always likes to remind us that past performance is no guarantee of future results. That may be true. However, although it is no guarantee, past performance is a pretty good predictor of what may happen in the future. That's why sports handicappers and portfolio managers analyze reams of data to make predictions. Trends are real, and although they may not continue in a straight line, they will generally continue in the current direction.

So, I make predictions. Every year, I try to forecast what I envision for the upcoming regulatory year based on current and past events. It's an imperfect science, but I have done pretty well. Last year, for example, I went 4-6, a .400 batting average, which would get me in the Baseball Hall of Fame. I am especially proud of those results given the uncertainty heading into the first year of the Trump administration. The prior year, I went 4-3-3 (ties claimed for events that were very close). In 2015, I went 6-4. Check out the blog for my predictions and track record.

Last year, I hit on my predictions concerning the fiduciary rule, whistleblowers, state enforcement, and individual liability. I accurately predicted that the

Trump administration would delay implementation of the DOL fiduciary rule rather than completely eliminate it[31]. I also accurately predicted the continued growth and expansion of the whistleblower program as key to SEC enforcement initiatives. I also foresaw that significant cases would be brought by the state regulators and that the SEC would bring significant cases against corporate executives. I have dealt with each of these trends in this book.

However, I was completely wrong on three of my predictions for 2017, and three others may have been premature. The SEC did not propose third-party compliance exams. We still think this might ultimately happen, but Jay Clayton has shelved this initiative. Neither Congress nor the SEC raised the private fund sponsor registration threshold above $150 million, even though both parties (as well as Barney Frank himself) support this change. Congress also failed to increase SEC penalty caps. FINRA did not become the primary regulator for retail advisers and broker-dealers, although this could still happen depending on the outcome of the SEC's proposed best interest standard. Because the equity markets continued to surge, firms did not begin to accelerate outsourcing. Our prediction about bond pricing may ultimately prove accurate, as the fixed income markets have begun to struggle with liquidity issues.

I only lay out my track record to build my bona fides in the prediction game. With my prophecies behind me, here are some predictions for the investment management regulatory world for the upcoming twelve months:

1. More states will adopt fiduciary rules. Nevada has already adopted a uniform fiduciary standard in the wake of the DOL's delay. We expect other states (e.g., California, New York, and Connecticut) to follow. This may become more likely now that the Fifth Circuit has vacated the DOL fiduciary rule, and the SEC has proposed the watered-down best interest standard for retail brokers.

2. The SEC will commence significant cybersecurity enforcement actions. The staff has done a sweep and issued guidance, although we have not yet seen significant enforcement actions. We have already seen a $35 million fine levied against Yahoo for failing to disclose a breach that occurred in 2014.

---

31   I did not however predict that the 5th Circuit would completely vacate the rule!

3. There will be cases alleging C-suite wrongdoing in private equity. The SEC Enforcement Division has focused on the private equity industry for the last couple of years. Given its interest in prosecuting senior executives to deter unlawful conduct, expect a couple of big cases against private equity execs.

4. FINRA will bring actions against firms for hiring bad brokers. Rather than simply prosecute the brokers, FINRA will dedicate some enforcement resources to firms that fail to screen them out, thereby making it a firm responsibility.

5. SEC and/or FINRA will bring cases alleging inadequate branch office supervision. Both regulators have expressed concerns about remote office supervision. Enforcement cases will ensure the industry's attention.

6. The SEC will commence significant marketing/advertising cases. Seemingly out of the blue, the SEC warned advisers about misleading marketing and advertising claims. We are assuming that OCIE is uncovering a lot of problems.

7. The SEC will propose a rewrite of the custody rule. The custody rule has the right intent, but the rule itself is too open to interpretation and questions (see multiple FAQs). We think the Division of Investment Management will undertake a rewrite (although maybe this is just wishful thinking).

8. The SEC will propose cryptocurrency regulations. Bitcoin futures are increasingly volatile. The SEC has expressed its opinion that it should regulate cryptocurrency offerings. We expect some rules.

9. The SEC will adopt the re-proposed ETF rule[32]. Plain vanilla ETFs should have a rule that allows them to proceed without an exemptive order. The SEC proposed and abandoned such a rule several years ago. We anticipate that the SEC will finish the process this time.

10. Several RIAs will disclose deteriorating financial conditions. Because of the significant changes in Form ADV and SEC scrutiny of RIA

---

32   In December 2017, we predicted correctly that the SEC would re-propose the ETF rule. As of this writing, the proposal is in the comment period.

disclosure, we expect that more advisers will add disclosure about (or be charged with failures to properly disclose) negative financial events.

I will report how these predictions panned out on our website, although I am reminded of the late, great Casey Stengel, who once warned, "Never make predictions, especially about the future."

About the Author

Todd Cipperman is the founding principal of Cipperman Compliance Services (CCS). Since 2004, CCS and its affiliates have helped advisers, broker-dealers, and funds protect their franchises through the development, implementation, and operation of customized compliance programs that include ongoing review, testing, management, training, and regulatory response. CCS leverages the experience of a multi-disciplinary team and takes full accountability for its advice and services. You can find more information at www.cipperman.com

Mr. Cipperman has over 25 years of experience in the investment management and financial services industries. He has represented a wide range of investment management clients with a focus on distribution issues facing investment managers and broker-dealers. He previously served as general counsel of SEI Investments, a public mutual fund and financial technology firm, including its $65 Billion proprietary mutual fund family. He spent several years in private practice on Wall Street representing both buy and sell side clients in investment management and capital markets transactions.

He is a graduate of the University of Pennsylvania Law School and Cornell University.

Mr. Cipperman is the author of the "Our Take" Regulatory Alerts, which provide daily updates on important industry developments via e-mail. An archive can be found at http://cipperman.com/blog/.

He is married to his law school sweetheart and does his best to mentor two teenage daughters. He lives in Malvern, PA (and Ocean City, NJ in the summers).

Here is his contact information:

Todd Cipperman
Cipperman Compliance Services
480 E. Swedesford Road
Suite 220
Wayne, PA 19087
www.cipperman.com
tcipperman@cipperman.com
(610) 687-5320

 @cipperman

/todd-cipperman-7117073

67590091R00128

Made in the USA
Middletown, DE
13 September 2019